Tear the Page Out

What it takes to Innovate in a Bureaucratic Organization

CONTENTS

D1413430

"Life can be more than a straight shot, starting with your first job and ending with retirement. Think of life as a Series of Hoops. To make the most of it, you've got to be ready, and bold enough, to jump."

Rhea Chiles - Florida's Former First Lady

Tear the Page Out is dedicated to a true innovator – Rhea Chiles. Her unique way of looking at life's journey as a *Series of Hoops*, inspired me to abandon my linear career path as a practicing Architect and begin to see *Everything as just another Design Problem*. In sharing our innovative adventures together, I came to embrace three principles that continue to guide my life's pursuits:

Always be looking for the next chance to make a difference, always be ready to seize the moment, and always be bold enough to act when there is no guarantee of success.

FOREWORD

I never intended to work in a Bureaucracy, public or private. But most of my notable innovative accomplishes were achieved working in a state government agency, a public University, and a large publicly owned company, each a bureaucracy.

I started my career as an Architect, working by the rules of the free-enterprise system; competing for work, getting paid for services rendered. If things went well, I made lots of money. If things went bad, I skipped a paycheck and maybe even missed a car payment. It was an entrepreneurial small business where success was tied to performance and risk was embraced, not avoided.

1

But for two-thirds of my working life, I've been an entrepreneur, more properly termed an **intrapreneur***, successfully innovating <u>inside</u> of a large **bureaucratic organization.*** I am a testament to the fact that it can be done – that you can be innovative and do *meaningful work* despite the restrictions of a bureaucratic environment.

* Intrapreneur

An intrapreneur behaves like an entrepreneur while working within a large organization.

I've always been an innovator at heart, always seeing the status quo as something to dismantle and rebuild, or at least to reshape. Although I was trained as an Architect, I sought and found other opportunities to apply the essence of the problem solving skills I learned in the design studio. This book is about my fortunate and extraordinary experiences being an innovator and highlights *lessons learned* from my successes, struggles, and failures. Included are principles I have found to be essential, and the inherent consequences of the necessarily disruptive and often unwelcome nature of innovation – especially within a bureaucratic organization. I've been blessed to have had several distinct careers in which I could conceive and implement innovative ideas. Searching for opportunities to innovate is in my DNA. It's been one delightful, challenging, and sometimes bumpy ride.

* Bureaucratic Organization

A large public institution or private business operating on strict rules, moving from concept to completion step by step with reviews and approvals along the way, having substantial resources, both people and capital, and adequate time allotted to deliver a service or product.

I hope my experiences will inspire those who feel held back by the system, feel forced to accept the status quo, and eager to contribute if only given the chance. I want to assure those who feel trapped in a Bureaucracy not open to their innovative ideas, that they can overcome the friction of change and make a difference.

"Your time is limited, so don't waste it living someone else's life. Don't be trapped by dogma - which is living with the results of other people's thinking. Don't let the noise of others' opinions drown out your own inner voice. And most important, have the courage to follow your heart and intuition."

Steve Jobs

The lessons I've learned, innovating while working in a bureaucracy, will benefit you best if I first begin by sharing what contributed to my approach to innovating. By understanding my *DNA*, you'll be able to compare your background and circumstances to mine, and then apply the applicable *Lessons Learned* to your own unique situation.

1 MY DNA – WHAT MAKES ME TICK

I've always been extremely curious. And I've been accused of being audacious on more than one occasion, probably because my curiosity makes people feel they're being interrogated. When I see an opportunity for improvement, I'm willing to be disruptive and I can move forward without certainty of the outcome. When action is more critical than planning, I'm willing to improvise. These personality traits have shaped how I approach problem solving.

3

My Life's Non-linear path – Jumping Hoops

My first distinctive career was in the PRIVATE SECTOR. I was an Architect/Developer focused on designing great buildings. I then served in the PUBLIC SECTOR as the Deputy Chief of Staff in the Governor's Office and as a State Agency Head trying to Reinvent Government. I left government and joined ACADEMIA. While at the University, I worked to insure we all became lifelong learners. I also consulted with a major corporation, sharing lessons learned from my government service and advised a StartUp online company on what it takes for an entrepreneurial venture to launch and ultimately be successful.

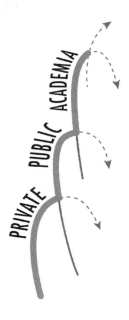

Jumping Hoops

In each sector I led innovative initiatives, some having high impact, some not. But even the initiatives of little consequence had value,

"... Think of life as a Series of Hoops. To make the most of it, you've got to be ready, and bold enough to jump."
Rhea Chiles

providing experiences that could be leveraged when launching future initiatives.

My Life's Circumstances

My ideas about innovation have been shaped partly by my life's circumstances. I was raised in a middle-class family in the South, I went to Catholic school, attended a public university, becoming a registered Architect at age 23 and, at 28, a principal in my own firm in Sarasota Fl. I've been happily

4

married for over 40 years and the father of four children. My family has never lived in a home I didn't design and build.

Those are the highlights. I strongly recommend you don't start down your path to innovation until you understand your DNA; until you know the course that best fits your passion, your skills, and your unique circumstances; until you understand yourself.

In addition to the circumstances of my life, my approach to problem solving, searching for innovative solutions, has been influenced by people I admire.

Those who Influenced My Thinking

Louis Kahn
Architect/Philosopher

VOLUME ZERO

Kahn was always searching for beginnings, what he called Volume Zero. He envisioned "that which is not yet made." I always try to begin formulating an innovative idea by searching for Volume Zero.

I begin with Rhea Chiles. We worked side by side, becoming partners in innovation (I'll elaborate later). But others, I have only known by reading their words and studying their works. Although I have learned from many, I will mention just a few. In reflecting on those who have influenced me, the list would include giants like Ben Franklin and Steve Jobs. But as it happens, being an Architect has exposed me to Architects and their works, so I guess we share a common perspective. I *get* them.

First – Louis Kahn. He was one of the great Architects of the 20th century but I see him more as a Philosopher. His ideas have influenced, and continue to shape, my thinking. He said **"A great**

5

building must begin with the unmeasurable, must go through measurable means when it is being designed and in the end must be unmeasurable." I never begin implementing an innovative idea without having his inspiring words in mind. I read his words and study his works regularly.

Richard Saul Wurman's writings have also influenced my thinking. He created the TED conference (Google it if you haven't heard about it) and was a student of Kahn's at the University of Pennsylvania. He had an impact on my

Richard Saul Wurman
Architect/Writer

approach to problem solving. Particularly his book – *Information Anxiety* – influenced how I go about organizing information. He said information can be organized in only five ways – Category, Time, Location, Alphabet, and Continuum. I'm always distilling stuff to a list and then sorting by continuum – Greatest to Least.

Information can be organized in only five ways -

- **Category**
- **Time**
- **Location**
- **Alphabet**
- **Continuum**

A third innovator who had an impact on me was Bruce Goff. He influenced the way I'm willing to start over, to jump from one good idea to the next even better idea. Bruce was seen as perhaps the most "*Fearless*" Architect of the 20th century. His designs used throw-away materials such as pie pans, metal pipes, ropes, bottles, and cans. Some would call him a *master at improvisation*. Each of his works were unique, as if he had discovered a completely new way to solve each design challenge he faced. I admire that.

To *Reinvent the Wheel Every Monday Morning*

"The Artist must have a wide vocabulary of digested and assimilated experiences inherited and acquired. He must have an unlimited capacity and range for feeling, an **insatiable curiosity and boundless enthusiasm."**

Bruce Goff

has been part of my approach to problem solving since I became an Architect. I believe now, more than ever, to "thrive in the age of acceleration" (Tom Friedman - *Thanks for Being Late*), you must, as Steve Jobs said, *"think different"* and I would add *"every Monday morning."*

These innovators, one I knew face-to-face, the others only by their work, helped make me become a better innovator. So how about you? Besides your life's circumstances, who shaped your vision for innovation?

I've found it useful for me to know my DNA. Self-reflection is invaluable to discover your unique *point of beginning*. You'll also need to identify the people who have had an impact on

"You can never learn anything that is not a part of yourself."

Louis Kahn

the way you think. Some you know personally, who share your passion, who get you. Others you have never met, but you have studied their work, read their books, and made their ideas yours. Do you have these type of people in your life? Have you taken the time to reflect on how they have shaped your approach to problem solving? I recommend you do.

When Things Don't Work, Refocus and Work Harder

While in college studying Architecture I was taught design started with a Blank Sheet. All possibilities were open. This basic Design training is foundational to my approach to innovation.

The Blank Sheet Thinking phase is the most difficult but also the most exciting – you're creating something from nothing. Once the design concept has been established, the real work begins – the implementation phase. This is where you struggle with the realities, as an Architect or an Innovator – the unique circumstances including the budget, the context, the customer requirements, the market demand, and more.

"You only understand information relative to what you already understand."
Richard Saul Wurman

But even if everything falls into place, not many great ideas actually get executed. Frequently, the practicing Architect's design concept never moves past a sketch. It remains, what Architects call a Paper Project, just a 100 gigabyte file stored digitally in a cold dark room. Many factors can kill a project, but Architects will often fall short if they don't *walk in their clients shoes.*

For Best Results, Make Their Goals Your Goals <1

Early in my practice of Architecture, I learned my most creative designs, documented with the most detailed construction documents, did not ensure the final result would be an award-winning project, or even that the building would be built. A majority of my clients were Developers and, frankly, they were mostly in it for the money. They weren't opposed to an outstanding work of Architecture as long as Outstanding would contribute to improving their bottom line.

I thought I could educate my clients, convincing them that a great building

TakeAway <1

Know what your customer wants

You'll seldom sell your innovative idea with a pitch that doesn't address the "What's in it for me?" question.

If you want your idea to be implemented, you must speak the language of the target market.

was its own reward. That was dumb. I soon realized I had a better chance to have my best work built if I mastered their language – the Pro Forma – the analysis of the money that included their Net Profit.

To capture their attention, I needed to study how projects were funded, how the Income and Expense projections were researched and structured, and how money flowed over time. As I began to become more knowledgeable about the numbers, I was fascinated and started to see the beauty in planning and managing cash flow. It was math, *just another design problem.*

I began to offer clients designs based on the numbers. I could see they were not particularly concerned with the Look and Layout of the building as long as the design was subjugated to the cash flow analysis. Looking good was ok as long as they hit the profit margin they were after. As I mastered the numbers, I started to exert more influence over the client, increasing the likelihood the building might get built the way I had envisioned. As I grew my expertise, I could see the next Hoop. I realized total control was better than just influencing my clients. To deliver the best built environment I was going to take a Leap. I was going to control as much as possible: the design, the budget, financing, sales, and construction. I was going to become the Developer.

2 "MORE RISK, MORE REWARD"

Developers start with a Blank Sheet – Raw Land. They translate their vision into a final product based on projections generated from assumptions (translation – their *Best Guess*). Developers have all the essential risk taking characteristics of an entrepreneur. I understood leaving my relatively safe, fee-driven world as an Architect to enter the unpredictable Development business would be challenging, but I was ready to give up my predictable path in order to have more control.

I began to test the waters, first with my own office building, then a few more office buildings. I now had the most control possible for a relatively small project. I had gained the confidence to think bigger, to ramp it up.

I had done an office building and a personal residence for a client who lived in Tallahassee. He owned a very successful communications business and, partly as a result of his father being a US Senator, he had an expansive network of contacts. His business,

Conference room of my firm's new office building

staffed by a team of skilled professionals, was almost on autopilot. He was looking for a new challenge and so was I. It turned out the development business would fit the bill for us both. If we found an exciting venture, we agreed we would join forces and jump in. He wasn't one to dilly-dally. Two weeks later, he called, "I found a deal we can't pass up."

He had forged ahead, getting an option on a site a block from the Capitol on Adams Street, a ground-zero location. He wasn't sure what we should do with the property, but he knew it was a winner. I was a little more cautious and suggested I do a feasibility study. Initially, we both assumed renting offices to lobbyists made the most sense. But after running the numbers, I determined the highest and best use was a hotel. It would generate more revenue and would have significant tax advantages. I thought – *Why rent by the year when you can rent by the day?* That sounded pretty clever, yet it turned out

Hotel in downtown Tallahassee

running a hotel was really complicated. But we were young and in the wild enthusiasm phase; we left the details till later.

I developed a package so we could test the investor market. He tapped his network of relationships and the response was favorable. He was confident the projected upfront capital required, about a million dollars, could be secured. Next, we needed to see if the market agreed with the potential investors. I had an appraiser gather data on rooms available vs. rooms needed. The market report indicated the demand for hotel room-nights exceeded the supply, especially in the market we would target – the high end. We made the decision to go for it. (This was well before Air B&B which would, in the future, erode the high end market and depress the value of the hotel.)

A year later we were ready to unveil our creation – the Governor's Inn, a 40-room Bed & Breakfast in the shadow of the Capitol. My partner, with the help of his dad, had managed to get Florida's four living governors to attend the Ribbon Cutting. It became a block party, Tallahassee's event of the year.

Ribbon-Cutting for the Governor's Inn. Left to Right – LeRoy Collins, Reubin Askew, Bob Graham, and Farris Bryant.

11

The Fateful Night that Changed My Life's Path

The evening before the opening ceremony, Senator Chiles and his wife, Rhea, hosted a dinner at the Governor's Club, across the street from our new hotel. In attendance were the four past governors and their first ladies, my business partner, myself, and our wives. It was a night to remember with old political stories the currency of the evening's conversation. At that dinner, I met someone who would change the trajectory of my life's path – Rhea Chiles. I had no idea what adventures I would share with this *Force of Nature*.

After the hotel opening, my wife and I headed back to Sarasota and I settled into designing projects and running my Architecture business. It was a comfortable life.

Several months passed before I saw Rhea again. The Senator had retired and they had moved to Anna Maria Island, just up the coast, about 30 minutes from Sarasota. I invited them to lunch at one of my favorite bay-front restaurants and to my delight, they accepted. As we ate, Rhea shared with me some fascinating stories about her brother, a Miami Architect whose firm was recognized as one of the most prominent in the State. It was obvious she admired him and had an interest in Architecture. Her energy was contagious and I was determined to get to know her better. I invited her to visit my office in Sarasota. She seemed open to the idea and said she would call.

I heard from her two days later. She said she was in town and would drop in. Within the hour, I was giving her the office tour. I had been working on a new idea and I took the opportunity to get her take. Her reaction was *"over-the-top"* positive. She believed it could be a game-changer, a fantastic technology tool that would put design in the hands of anyone hoping to build a new home. What she said next was really a surprise – she asked if she could help. WOW, I could hardly believe my ears. I jumped at the chance to have her magic sprinkled over my idea.

Within a month, she had an office in my building and her first computer (a Mac) on her desk. She was not a spectator; she was a first-string player

and she, like me, believed **Dream Home was going to change the way America builds in the 21ˢᵗ Century.**

3 LEAVING THE NEST TO CHASE THE DREAM

Creating Dream Home Designer began with asking a question that has always been a challenge in the business of design and construction: how to get clients from concept to construction – Fast. **<2**

The Architect had always employed a yellow pad to jot down the client's ideas and a roll of sketch paper to rough out early design options. Even today, where construction documents are 100% computer based, designers still frequently start with a hand-drawn sketch. I still feel the connection between the eye and the hand is more "true" than the eye and the mouse – but this could just be me resisting the new way.

13

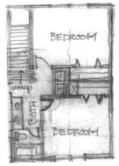

Typically, two or three meetings would occur, and then the Architect would bring in a builder to put some preliminary numbers to the conceptual plans. There would be a couple more meetings, and then the Go or No-Go decision would be made.

The odds of proceeding were low, maybe 50% at best – assuming the client was thrilled with the design solution and the estimated cost was in range. But both the Architect and Builder were spending way too much time trying to land a client rather than producing construction documents and breaking ground. I believed the technology was available to completely reinvent the process of moving from concept to construction, making it much more engaging for the client and efficient for the Architect and Builder. Just a little heads up – my assumption that the technology was ready was a little premature.<3

The result of reinventing the process – more clients would sign a contract and move forward. I wanted to put the power of design in the customers' hands. The feeling of control, of getting exactly what they wanted, the thrill of Designing their own Dream Home, that would be a game-changer.

TakeAway <3

Don't get ahead of the technology

Know the current state of Technology and be able to envision where it's going. It's extremely difficult to predict where technology will be in the future and how it will impact a product or service. If you sense a big leap coming soon, you'll need to factor in the potential impact.

The system had three key elements:

1. The computer to display the customer's design choices

2. The home design disks with 64 options including the pricing

3. The CAD working drawings delivered express mail in 48 hrs.

At this point, I had 2 partners, Rhea and my hotel development partner (her son) the communication wizard from Tallahassee. He had found an investor and I had pulled together a team that could write the code for the software and generate the CAD drawings. The vision of Dream Home Designer was now clear and the resources were in place to make it happen.

We wanted to use a computer and our custom home software disks to offer a library of home options to anyone ready to design their own dream home. Our system produced an instant printout that included the home's front elevation, floor plan, a list of features, and the price.

Once the customer made a commitment, the CAD construction documents could be generated immediately and sent to the builder by express mail.

We wanted customers to take control and builders to be freed from endless, time-consuming design meetings, to get on with what they do best, and how they make a living – building houses.

We had put together some well-crafted visuals for the marketing package. All that was left was framing the words to complement the images. I was sure I could write the promotional copy we needed.<4 My marketing-savvy partner had someone who he insisted should do the writing. She was already scheduled to come over the next morning to talk with me.

I said OK but knew it was a waste of time. I spent the evening writing out the vision and by the scheduled meeting with the professional writer, I was armed with the written words I was sure she would love. We talked for two hours, I was exhausted. She may have been as curious as I was. She asked if she could have my version for reference (I later realized she was just being diplomatic). I said absolutely, thinking she was just going to tweak my work a bit. A week later, I got her draft.

Promotional Text - Dream Home Designer

DRAFT

A computerized architectural digest finally brings custom de-sign to the regular builder and buyer. Its breakthrough tech-nology, simple to use and dramatic to look at, not only irresist-ibly draws buyers to your business, but gives you instantane-ous pricing and incredibly fast working drawings for hundreds of custom homes. Dream Home Designer forever solves one of the builder's most frustrating problems: How to get customers from creative decisions to construction fast.

When buyers aren't sure what they want, can't visualize plans, or ask for changes and then decide a week later that they're too expensive, your front-end, non-billable time mounts and mounts. You're not building houses, you're not making money, and you may even lose a sale.

But when – in your office and in a matter of hours – you can choose from hundreds of custom-home plans, change design elements with the touch of a button, watch a composite drawing take shape before their eyes, and get an instant tabulation of prices, you're on your way to a signed contract . . . and to the building site.

I read the first draft looking for my version. It had vanished, and good riddance. I was mesmerized with her word-smithing. She had painted a picture that captured the magic of Dream Home Designer (DHD).

Making the Dream Come True

We now had a compelling narrative of my vision to sell the idea DHD would change the way America builds in the 21st century. It was time to test the market.

Lucky for us, the National Home Builders Conference was scheduled for Orlando in 90 days. It would be the perfect venue to launch Dream Home. Our marketing whiz-kid got the former Miss Florida to work our booth at the conference. We had a fantastic product to draw the crowd, I didn't see why we needed Miss Florida. OK, I missed that one, too.

We had a booth in the exhibition hall, and a 30-minute breakout session. Miss Florida had studied our product and had wonderful sales skills in both formats. Maybe, as they say, it is all about marketing. We presented a short video at the breakout session targeting our custom home builder audience.

We wanted to convey one idea – why they couldn't build another home without having the Dream Home Designer System.

The outcome was overwhelming. We sold 32 systems in less than an hour. We were now convinced our sales and marketing approach should include demonstrating the system and the promotional video. (Oh yea, and the former Miss Florida was asked, and agreed to be our official spokesperson.)

We were out of the gate like a rocket and could already see the finish line. Being off to a great start was certainly a plus, but I soon began to temper my enthusiasm.

I had been in this spot before, when my Hotel project's grand opening was grand, but after 30 days, room rentals were abysmal. Why? The simple answer was we hadn't put together any kind of a marketing plan. Like the Hotel, Dream Home's unveiling was fantastic, but, here again, we didn't have a well crafted plan to ramp up sales. We sounded the alarm and did the obvious – get our sales team calling the hundreds of customer contacts we had gathered at the conference. A few weeks went by and we had only sold two new systems. It was clear that phone calls weren't the answer. But What? We realized we needed to do what had worked at the conference, hands on demos. The sales team hit the road charged with calling on prospects to make face to face presentations. But we had missed our chance. **<5**

TakeAway <5

Be aware of how the price tag and learning curve can discourage buyers

But when up-front cost is too high and it takes too long to master the product's use, buyers won't buy.

Strive to make the initial cost as low as possible and the product very simple to use.

During his campaign for Governor, Lawton debated with his opponent – Jeb Bush. Lawton was trailing. The moderator asked when was he gonna make his move. Lawton's reply - "The Old He-Coon walks just before the light of dawn" - baffled Jeb.

Lawton, the Old He-Coon, made his move and WON!

Reality had set in with the potential buyers. They loved the idea of DHD but realized the System's upfront cost was just too high. One contractor told our salesman he had calculated it would take at least three years to recoup his investment. This was a fact we had unfortunately overlooked. If we could have offered renting the System, that may have helped to overcome the upfront cost challenge. But that was water over the dam. We knew Dream Home was a great idea but we had underestimated the *cost of ownership* barrier.

In addition, Dream Home had another obstacle it couldn't overcome – the learning curve was too steep. We were totally convinced that anyone would find the DHD System simple to use, but we forgot something to validate our assumption – actual users Testing the System!

Dream Home Designer never became the national sensation we had envisioned. But there was a most beneficial personal outcome – the DHD experience would be the key to my next career opportunity.

Lawton Chiles was not good at being a retired Senator. He turned in his days of chillin' on the beach for the campaign trail. He had decided to run for Governor. He and Rhea left for Tallahassee to announce his candidacy. I assumed that I would not be hearing from Rhea anytime soon. Maybe after the election. I quickly realized how much I missed the excitement. But then I got an unexpected call. "Get up here – we need your help." It was Rhea.

What I had learned creating the Dream Home system would be key to implementing a campaign Head Quarters computer network and a statewide communications system for a political campaign.<6 This talent was my ticket to the ball park. Lawton had a special way of connecting with the people – and the people responded by electing him Governor of the State of Florida.

I was part of the farm team that had worked on the campaign. I had not thought past winning but when Lawton said he and Rhea would like me to join his team, I accepted without hesitation. It was the beginning of a new life for me and my family. I didn't know then, but I would never be a practicing Architect again.

Learning the Ways of the Political World

I was filled with anticipation, ready for the next Hoop. But being a newbie to

TakeAway <6

Innovation breeds Innovation

Once you get started launching innovative initiatives, you'll find new inspirations come more easily. You may think of a spinoff or an add-on to your idea. As you go through the implementation process for one idea, you'll see new opportunities. Make sure you stay in the creative mode, be ready to leverage your first working innovation into the next new thing (e.g. remember, Amazon started as an on-line book seller).

the ways of politics, a private sector player who didn't know the game, I had a lot to learn – and quickly. The Governor had served for two terms as a U.S. Senator and recruited many of his Senate senior staff to Tallahassee. I assumed we were all on the Governor's team and they would give me a crash course on how to survive in the political world. Wrong!

This Washington clan spoke the language of politics and were schooled in the ways of the political wheeler-dealers that infested the Capitol. But they weren't willing to welcome an interloper with such a personal connection to the Governor to join the team. The Washingtonians didn't like anyone even speaking to the Governor without going through them. I soon realized that trying to get in their good graces would be fruitless. I decided I needed to go to the top to get my marching orders directly. Luckily, I got an invite to lunch the next day with the Governor Elect.

A small group met for fried chicken at Nick's, an institution in Tally. As we left, walking the three blocks back to the Capitol, I asked Lawton what he wanted me to do. He stopped, looked at me and said, "Find Meaningful Work." I must admit, I was looking for something a little more specific, but that was it. Where could I go with that?

No Assigned Seats

At the time, I didn't get the power of his message. I was expecting some defined role he wanted me to play, some specific assignment. But I soon realized what he had given me – I had **a Ticket to the ball park, But there were no assigned seats**. It would be up to me to take my place at the table.

My arrival in the capital city had been delayed by a few days. Turns out, late ain't good. To the Washingtonians, I was a non-player. They had no intention of letting me in the game.

They had all the turf, leaving me with No Title, No Office, and one more problem – no parking space. It was unspoken, but their obvious preference was for me togo back home to Sarasota.

I was getting concerned about my decision to leave Sarasota. I had a well-oiled Architecture machine, a house on the Bay, a nice boat in my slip and a Corvette in the garage. That was gone, Tallahassee was now home. I had put my trust in the Old He-Coon, and on that count, I had no regrets.

I went over the challenges in my mind: I didn't know anything about politics, I was seen as a know-nothing outsider by both the Tallahassee and Washington insiders, and I had No Turf. Then I listed my advantages:

Lawton had giving me a bulletproof vest as long as I followed his one rule: "Don't do anything immoral or illegal." And the First lady, Rhea Chiles, had become a strong ally and spoke both architecture and politics. She knew the political ways of Tallahassee and would be my translator and co-conspirator to implement the Governor's agenda.

I slept on my situation and by morning I had pulled myself together. I decided to move forward, to take one step at a time. First, I needed some of the basics, a place to work and park my car.

I turned to my strongest ally, the First Lady. She got me started, offering me a small storage room that I could convert to my office. It was not in the Capitol, but, as it turned out, it was an upgrade.

Because of its proximity, my storage-room office allowed me an opportunity to chat with Lawton frequently and occasionally be invited for breakfast with him and Rhea. I also got a parking space. My new office was in the lower floor of the Governor's Mansion.

I would begin each day in my Mansion office and walk ten blocks down a shaded Adams street to the Capitol. I found

 the walk of great benefit, giving me time to get focused on my goal for the day and when walking back to the Mansion, I could collect my thoughts and think of what to share with the Governor. He was usually in the gym in the afternoon when I got to my office. He would drop by to get my take on the day. He was briefed by the staff in the Capitol most mornings. But my report was not sanitized, not just the facts (as the staff saw it) but the feel of how we were "making a difference".

Having an office and a place to park was a confidence-builder. Getting a sanctioned job would be a much bigger challenge. Rhea couldn't help me (yet) with a job title, but for now, I was happy with my unofficial position working out of my storage-room office. It helped me to maintain my outsider status and gave me authority to participate in anything – I was the Governor's Guy with an office in the Mansion. I took my positioning with pride, I had a ticket to the ball park, and there were no assigned seats. Also, there was no staff meeting that I considered off-limits.

I arrived at the Capitol each morning already having read the daily schedule and selecting the meetings I planned to attend (some saw it as crashing). Many early morning meetings were in the Governor's Conference room. I'd show up a few minutes before everyone arrived and took a seat at the table, always the least prominent, but at the table. Once the meeting got going I would listen for an

State Capitol

assignment I could volunteer for and speak up – "I'll do that." Sometimes I was squeezed out by a staff member who, to be fair, was more suited for the assignment. But I always left with something to do. I began to see that no one was going to ask for my help or give me something important to do. It was a bit audacious but I adopted a new mantra – power is taken, not given.

This went on for several weeks with me having no institutional power and no troops. I was a one-man band and I eventually concluded, I was just keeping busy, not doing real Meaningful Work.

Power is Taken, Not Given

I came to realize, to get to do work that was actually mean-ingful, I had to have institutional credentials and staff to get substantial work done. I bolted out of bed the next morning with a brilliant idea.

TakeAway <8

Play the role expected

To move forward, you may need to focus on what the market sees as your expertise.

It may lead to bigger things. If the door is open – walk in.

I had, along with my brother and our friend from Apple, configured and installed the computer network for the campaign. I had creds in the tech space that could be leveraged. <8

I had met the Governor's office Director of Technology a few times. She was a holdover from the previous regime and it was obvious she had no interest in our mission. She had ten employees and was responsible for the computer hardware, software infrastructure, and the network for the Governor's office. Her view of desktop support was to keep the mainframe and green screen terminals up and running. My view was the office needed to Leap forward, to put a network-connected computer on every desk – from support staff to unit directors – and begin to leverage the power of teamwork by sharing information.

Run Till Tackled

I decided it was time for some disruption. I invoked the power is taken, not given principle. I would get rid of the Director and take over the Technology unit. I went to her office and advised her that if she agreed to resign, I would write a positive letter of recommendation and give her a six-month payout. She took my offer, cleaned out her desk, and was gone by 5 that afternoon. I now had a defined responsibility, a Title and troops to execute a mission to improve the IT services in the Governor's office. With the position also came an office and a parking space in the Capitol complex.

It took several months, but the Tech unit moved the Governor's office off the mainframe and onto servers in our newly constructed server room. We scrapped the green screens and put both MACS and PC's on a shared network. The feedback confirmed that we had made a difference, giving the Governor's team powerful tools to do their job. But I could see that the Tech unit would not be able to do any reinventing for a while. The unit was moving into maintenance mode and I was ready for a new challenge.

5 WITH SUCCESS COMES OPPORTUNITY

Just Kill Something

A year had passed. It was our first Christmas in Tally and my wife and I had joined Lawton and Rhea for after dinner drinks at the Governor's mansion. Lawton, who told me I should "Find Meaningful Work" but gave no direct orders, looked at me and said "My office operation is a mess, I thought you were the process expert." Rhea glanced over at me with *the look* – she was sending me a message, here's your chance to take a Leap. I took the hint and said "Governor, I can fix it but I'd need more authority. I'd need to be the Deputy Chief of Staff."

*"I live by two credos: **If you don't ask, you don't get**. And most things don't work."*

Richard Saul Wurman

He looked down at me over his reading glasses. He stared intensely and didn't utter a word, but I got the message (at least that's how I took it). He didn't want me to develop a plan for his review, he wanted me to fix it. **<9** In *Cracker speak*, he was saying *just kill something* – get it done. How – that was up to me. My mind was racing all night. I didn't get much sleep. The next morning, ready or not, I had to make my move.

26

I had a parking space under the Capitol but I left my car at the Mansion giving me time to think as I walked in. We already had a Deputy so I was not sure how to deal with that. Should I push him out like I did the Director of Technology? It worked then but I wasn't sure that was the right path now. In some areas, the current Deputy was doing a great job. He was managing the Governor's schedule which had never run better. But the overall operation was being run by a lot of campaign staff who weren't a good fit. They felt entitled and the Deputy wasn't prepared to take them on. I kept thinking "just kill something."

I came up with my plan of attack. My idea would be less disruptive than a firing and still give me the authority I needed to straighten out the operational issues.

I marched into the Chief of Staff's office and announced the Governor had asked me to fix any of the office's operational issues that needed fixin'. I said he wanted me to be the Deputy Chief of Staff but mainly focus on operations. My solution was to have two Deputies — Deputy of Operations and Deputy of Administration. I would focus on operations, the current Deputy would focus on administration. I laid it out and could see the pitch was working. This was not a hard decision for the Chief of Staff. He had no interest in operations; he was a political animal and was more than happy to dump the problems on me.

He had run the campaign and his passion was politics – getting the Governor's agenda through the legislature. He said "Fine. Just go down to the HR guy and get a new position established. One more thing, you'll need to break the news to our Deputy." I said I'd do it. I took care of the bureaucratic HR stuff first, getting a position established. Then I headed for the current Deputy's office.

He knew things were not running smoothly and felt a shakeup could be coming, so when I showed up he assumed the worst. Before he could say a word, I quickly dispelled the notion that he was out. I said "The Governor has no intention of letting you go. He just felt you were spread too thin and thought I could be some help." We talked for over an hour and I left with the current Deputy becoming the Deputy of Administration and me holding a new job – Deputy of Operations.

6 THE POWER OF INSTITUTIONAL AUTHORITY

I now had the institutional authority and a mandate (OK, implied mandate) from the Governor to streamline the operation.<10 We were beginning our second year in office, and still hadn't matched the right talent to the right task. Over the course of six months I reduced the office staff by 30%. Most were sent to jobs they'd be good at in one of the Governor's Agencies. Some were recruited by private companies, usually with a pay increase; a few left government service, returning home with a glowing letter about their service; most reconnecting with their previous jobs. In concert with the reductions in staff and associated costs, I gave the

TakeAway <10

Large enterprises are more susceptible to change from the inside

Being inside, but not vested in the established order, gives you the advantage of participating in the daily change process, different than an outside consultant.

high-performing workers, 18 staff, salary increases and still cut total salary costs. I had made the operational changes needed with as little disruption as possible. In implementing change, you need to remember that those you hurt, especially unjustly, can later hurt you.

Similar to the work I had done in IT, deploying a modern computer network, the job of reorganizing was over. There would be, of course, the day-to-day work of being the Deputy but I was anxious for a new challenge. Without warning, my wish was granted.

7 CRISIS REQUIRES IMPROVISATION

I felt good about what had been done internally. The operational issues in the Governor's office had been addressed and things were running smoothly. I was getting comfortable with the Deputy Chief of Staff's role and knew what my job responsibilities included. But that was about to change. Hurricane Andrew struck.

At 4:45AM on August 24th, 1992, Hurricane Andrew made landfall in south Florida as a category 5 storm. Florida has always been a target for hurricanes, but this was not the run of the mill storm – this was a category 5, the highest rating, with winds reaching 165 miles per hour.

The National Guard was activated and sent to maintain order and do what could be done to save lives and provide essential food and shelter. The Governor's office mobilized State agencies to assist in the recovery efforts. The Federal government authorized FEMA to coordinate their efforts with the State. It was an "All hands on deck" situation. From reports we were getting, the damage was extensive and the first responders were overwhelmed.

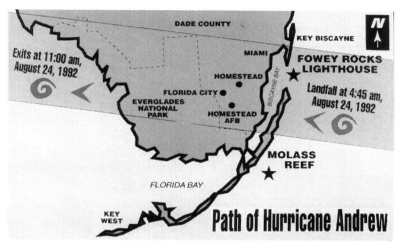

Path of Hurricane Andrew

Exits at 11:00 am, August 24, 1992

Landfall at 4:45 am, August 24, 1992

It would take months, more likely years, to recover – and it was going to take a lot of money.

In Washington, President H.W. Bush ordered an assessment to determine the amount of funding the Federal government would provide. In just 48 hours, the White House released their initial funding commitment. The total damage was put at approximately $6 billion. Meanwhile, at the State level, the Governor's Office had begun its own analysis and determined the cost to be much higher – almost double the White House estimate. This was going to be a two-front war. In addition to attacking the natural disaster, the Governor would lead the charge to secure the needed recovery funds from Washington.

The Governor, when he was serving as Chair of the Senate Budget committee in Washington, had mastered the funding game. He still had friends in this political world and requested an audience with the Senate to present Florida's case. The Governor knew Senate leadership would play an important role in determining the amount of dollars provided to address this natural disaster.

It was obvious the Chiles name still had pull in Washington. A meeting was set for the following week – just ten days out. The game was on. Everyone in the Governor's office was standing ready to do whatever needed to deal with the two challenges. A large contingent was sent to south Florida to help coordinate the effort on the ground. I was to stay in Tallahassee to keep the trains running on time.

I knew the Governor would be speaking to his old colleagues, Senators who had respect for Lawton and remembered his time in the Senate with fondness. They'd want to help, but they had many competing interests for funds; so even with the best personal chemistry, corroborating evidence would be important. I knew the Governor's planning and budget team was already putting together the numbers and that would be critical to provide a credible analysis. But I envisioned he would also need visuals with simple data-points to tell the story and illustrate the scope of the destruction.

The pitch needed to be from the heart and no one was better than Lawton for that. But I felt sometimes the right props can help to crystallize a story. Helping with the visual props was a task I would be good at.

I managed to get 5 minutes with the Governor and quickly laid out my idea; I would put together some presentation materials that he could use to support his conversation with his former colleges. I proposed setting up a skunkworks operation to expedite the process and run parallel to the other work being done by his budget office staff. I understood that the key funding request documents would be authored by the budget experts. But I wanted to portray the disaster visually. It would be his call, use it or not, but I said I'd like to give it a try. He said fine. In my mind I heard him say "just kill something."

I got some space in a building across the street from the Capitol to house the skunkworks. I felt like a StartUp working out of a garage. I began to put together the plan, the talent, and the resources. In 10 days the Governor would be in Washington for the meeting. I allocated 7 days to get the presentation ready. My guess was it would be at least 16-hour days and lots of order-out pizza (no beer – just coffee).

There wouldn't be time for a planning committee (luckily). My instinct was the presentation would be a prop for the Governor to tell his story about the devastation of the hurricane. The presentation would be a visual complement to his words but also highlight the financial impact of the disaster.

My plan started with what not to do. No technology, no PowerPoint. That was not Lawton's style. I knew it had to be simple but also compelling. I considered alternatives. Maybe have some Andrew victims, just average citizens, join Lawton and testify. Maybe get the mayor of Homestead to share his community's experience. Or maybe use video or photos to capture the devastation. The presentation would be restrained by the time allotted for the Senate meeting, 30 minutes max. Also, the flow would need to be controlled and staged for maximum impact. And perhaps the most important – telling the story with compassion. We already had the best person for that – Lawton. I nixed bringing additional speakers.

We would use still pictures. That would be the simplest and least likely to get screwed up. I realized the best approach would be to simply present before-and-after shots of the impact area. Then we would compare the value of the property and structures before the storm to the values after the storm. I liked the idea a lot. It seemed simple and direct. But where could I get before-and-after photos? In a flash I thought – satellite images.

To get before and after images from space, there was only one reliable source – NASA. Images from miles above the path of destruction would be dramatic.

To make this work, the NASA Director would need to make our request a priority. We were in luck. The Director reported to the Vice President, Dan Quayle, and one of the Governor's staff while he served in Washington, was now on Quayle's staff. The fix was on.

If we were going to get NASA to respond quickly, I knew we had to limit our request to just what we needed. The destruction covered 53 square miles. Time was limited so we needed to limit our request. I decided we would need to identify representative samples of the impacted areas. To be manageable, we requested sample aerials, each covering one square mile. We wanted pictures taken before and after in 4 categories: estuaries, suburban areas, agricultural land, and urban areas. When asked what size, I asked what's available? I could get from 8x10 to 44x44 inch. I was thinking of booklets, so 8x10's would be good. But then I had a flashback which changed my mind.

Several years ago I had taken my family to the Ringling Circus in Sarasota, housed under the "Big Top." In those days they were still setting up a gigantic tent. It was a sellout but I felt that we had plenty of room. But then the elephants came in. The stream of pachyderms seemed to go on for 10 minutes. The 3 rings were dominated by the size and quantity of the elephants. They took over the space – that was all you could see. You felt cramped. That would be the effect I would shoot for, to have the Governor's presentation dominate the space, to "fill" the Senate Chamber. ◄11

We put in our request for the largest pictures available, a before-and-after for each category for a total of 8 photos. We asked for two copies just in case. We quickly learned NASA was not a bureaucratic operation and we had the photos in 48 hours. Impressive. We now had the key resource needed for the visuals. Next we had to get the numbers.

This was something NASA didn't have. I asked the folks in the budget office if they knew of a source. No help. I called over to the Department of Revenue. After several transfers I got a lead. They said you might try the Dade county appraiser's office and gave me the number and a contact.

I really didn't know much about the appraisal process so I asked one of our policy coordinators in the budget office to call on behalf of the Governor. We provided the Sections (roughly one square mile to match our photos) needed for the County Appraiser's office to give us the property values before the storm. The Appraiser was glad to do whatever he could. We got the numbers on the properties in each Section in fewer than 8 hours – a hell of a turnaround. It was a lot of information and the data structure needed some work, but it gave us the base value we needed.

We had the before values but how would we get the after figures? Again, I turned to the budget office. They said I need to talk with the Environmental unit. They told me for this we would need someone who could interpret the damage – a

Cartographer. Another break: Our Geographical Information System (GIS) expert knew someone in Tampa who could do the analysis. After speaking to my new best friend, the Cartographer, and explaining what the Governor needed, he volunteered and was in Tallahassee the next day. The team was coming together.

The raw materials for the presentation's content were on site and the experts we needed to do the analysis were ready to go. Fortunately, the one last piece, the media presentation talent, already worked for me. The eMedia unit handled the Governor's presentations for press conferences and meetings around the State. They were up for the challenge.

By day 4 of the 7-day timeline, we had made good progress getting ready. Although we had just met some of our key skunkworks members, it was as if we had been working together for years. We all shared a sense of urgency to help in the recovery effort. It was now time to focus.

The main presentation would be on the 44"x44" boards using the original pictures from NASA. There would be eight 44"x44" boards, 4 sets - one before and one after for each category. The aerials would feature color overlays and accompanying text to explain the details. The first set was the before-and-after of the estuary; then the property used for agricultural; next the urban areas; and finally the suburban areas. We also would produce an 8.5x11 package, a takeaway for the Senators. But the 8 large posters were the key.

I tried to visualize the empty Senate chamber and then, when the 30-foot line of aerial photos were set on easels, how the room would be filled with the destruction of Hurricane Andrew.

As I had suspected, the team worked around the clock for the next three days. We all thought it was a minor miracle, but it was done. Most of the team crashed but there was still one more hurdle to jump – brief the Governor. I called and said I needed 10 minutes for him and Rhea to take a look at the presentation.

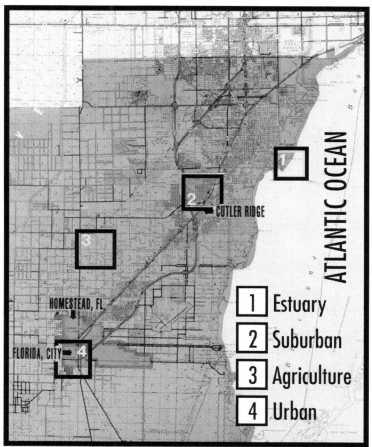

Map depicting the four categories of land usage that was sampled.

Our Cartographer and I brought the 8 boards and easels over to the Mansion. It was the evening before the Governor was leaving for Washington. He and Rhea had retired for the night but came down from the upstairs living quarters to the foyer where I had set up the boards. I walked them through the before-and-after trying to emphasize how we had linked the destruction to the lost value. Lawton smiled, gave me a thumbs-up, and without a word, headed upstairs to bed. Based on past interactions, I took that as a standing ovation. Rhea was more animated saying the photos would really help

Urban Zone presentation board with NASA satellite image depicting damage and summary of financial impact.

URBAN: HOMESTEAD/FLORIDA CITY

**Pre-Storm Value
(Improved Market Value)**

Residential	39,303,189
Commercial	4,272,184
Industrial	5,623,505
Agricultural*	285,602
Institutional	1,855,713
Government	5,962,955
Total	57,303,148

Estimated Loss

	75%	100%
Residential	29,477,391	39,303,189
Commercial	3,204,138	4,272,184
Industrial	4,217,629	5,623,505
Agricultural*	214,201	285,602
Institutional	1,391,785	1,855,713
Government	4,472,216	5,962,955
Total	42,977,360	57,303,148

Lawton tell the story. She gave me two thumbs-up. We left feeling we had done some meaningful work but had one more chore to handle. We drove to the State's aircraft hangar to deliver the boards and easels to be loaded on the plane in the morning. Our job was done.

All of us on the skunkworks team had been sleepless for days, living on takeout pizza and a steady flow of caffeinated soft drinks. When we got our senses back, the Washington meeting to secure the relief funding was just getting started. I spoke to the on-site staff to make sure they understood the staging. They assured me it would be set up as we had envisioned – a 30-foot line along a gentle arc, put in place after the Senators were in the chamber listening to the Governor's opening remarks. The meeting was scheduled for 30 minutes but it went long. All we could do now was wait.

I got a call from the Chief of Staff as the meeting concluded. His message was short – the Governor hit it out of the park and he told me to let you know the pictures were great. He was confident we'd get the money we needed.

I was not on the Washington negotiating team. The Governor called on the staff that worked for him when he was chair of the Senate budget committee. They were the Governor's experts and knew the funds allocation game. It took nearly two weeks but the Whitehouse revised its estimate. The new total cost of hurricane Andrew was set at $10 billion, less than the State's estimate of almost $12 billion but a lot higher than the initial $6 billion offered.

Many factors contributed to Florida's receiving the additional $4 billion. I like to think the visuals played a small part, I called it **the 4 billion dollar presentation**. But the one thing we all agreed on, our success was primarily due to the messenger – Lawton Chiles.

8 BECOMING THE TOP GOVERNMENT INTRAPRENEUR

Beginning the 3rd year in office, the Governor's first Chief of Staff joined a lobbying firm. A new Chief was brought in who was an old hand in government. He was a no-nonsense kinda' guy and had every intention of consolidating power under him. I could see the writing on the wall: My days as a freelance operator were coming to an end. <12

TakeAway <12

Don't overstay your welcome

Be good at reading the tea leaves. Identify the next Hoop – and jump.

Within 30 days of taking the helm, the Chief called me into his office to make his move. He knew I had a bulletproof vest, a special relationship with Lawton and Rhea, so he was too smart to fire me. But he had worked in the bureaucracy for years and he knew the best way to get rid of the competition – offer me a promotion.

A new Agency had just been created from merging the Department of Administration (DOA) with the Department of General Services (DGS). The new Agency, the Department of Management Services (DMS), needed a Secretary and he wanted to put my name forward to the Governor. He said take some time, discuss it with your wife, and let me know in a few days. I didn't need a few days, I said immediately "I'm your man." As I had done before, opportunity was knocking and I was ready to jump to the next Hoop.

"To succeed, jump as quickly at opportunities as you do at conclusions."
Ben Franklin

I would need to go through the formal selection process but I had a pretty good idea my biggest advocate had already done some lobbying. I knew the Governor was pleased I had his office operations working smoothly. But, as you may have gathered, he wasn't in the habit of verbalizing what he was thinking. I wanted this job, and if I was to be considered, I knew I would need to speak up. I could hear his words in my head, "It's a sad frog that won't croak in his own pond."

"Hide not your talents. They for use were made. What's a sundial in the shade?"
Ben Franklin

I decided to stop by the Mansion and talk to him face-to-face. I shared why I was sure I was the right man and ready to lead his new Agency. As expected, he peered over his readers and gave me the look. I left without comment, not quite sure how it had gone.

Once the basic job posting requirements were met, the application phase was over and the time for the public announcement of the new Secretary was set. I got a call from the scheduling office the day before the appointment went public, telling me to be on standby. This was a good sign. I had no official confirmation but got a call that night from Rhea. She said "Wear your best suit tomorrow." She didn't say I had it, but I was counting my chickens.

I got a call from the appointments office 12 hours before the press conference was scheduled. The Governor announced my appointment as Secretary the next day in the press room. As instructed, I had my best suit on (suits weren't me – so my best one was my only one). There were a few questions from the press but mostly the basics – name, home town, how do you spell your last name? I was a little surprised I didn't get grilled for being a crony. But no one brought it up.

I was confident, perhaps overly, that I was ready to take on this challenge and I wanted to go in with guns blazing. I was ready to "change the world." But I had gotten some advice about keeping my guns in their holsters and I was smart enough to listen (more on that later).

The job was going to be challenging, but incredibly exciting. I had what the Governor had encouraged me to find – "meaningful work." I sometimes try to recount my steps, asking how I got so lucky? I think the simple answer is what I had learned from Rhea –

Always be looking for the next chance to make a difference, Always be ready to seize the moment, and Always be bold enough to act when there is no guarantee of success.

9 INTRAPRENEURS NEED NOT APPLY

Don't Expect a Welcoming Party

I walked into what would be my new office not expecting the former DGS Deputy Secretary, now supposedly working for me, sitting behind my desk. I assumed he had come to welcome me onboard and ask what he could do to help. I missed that one. I missed it really bad. He stood up, and said "I can't believe they put you in charge; you have no idea how we do things."◄13

41

Then, he stormed past me and grumbled under his breath "You won't last six months." So at that moment it became apparent I would need to be more guarded. Over my first few weeks I found some folks were at least willing to listen, but it appeared upper management would do everything they could to defend the status quo.

In the Beginning, Hold your Cards Close

As I mentioned, I had gotten some good advice on how to get started. I started slowly, just getting a feel for the current basic procedures. No *Change Mandates*, no mass firings.<14 The Governor's office Chief of Staff had advised me not do anything for the first 90 days, just listen. He had been an Agency Head and served in many government positions over his career in state government.

I knew if he said it, I should pay attention. I followed his advice, listening to everyone from Division directors to administrative assistants, and kept my mouth shut as best I could (keeping my mouth shut is not my strong suit). I was building my knowledge database, starting to understand the culture, identifying what was working, what could be improved easily, and what would pose the biggest challenges.

TakeAway <13

Personal attacks can be brutal

Remember, it's not about you, it's about them. They'll act confused, then tell you why your idea won't work, and finally tell everyone you're crazy. Stay positive. Don't retaliate with insults.

TakeAway <14

Don't start with guns blazing

Don't expect for everyone to give you the "real" truth, but still listen before you roll out your vision.

Getting input from the current team may produce mixed results, but signaling that you will listen is important.

42

I was getting ready to play my cards. I had been formulating what I felt was a very innovative plan, and was eager to roll it out. I had given the initiative a title I felt was descriptive of the goal, moving the Agency from Regulator to Resource. Before the unveiling, I had an opportunity to get some public exposure of my thoughts on how government should work.

I was asked to write an editorial for the *Miami Herald*. I titled my article "Why can't government run like a business?"

At the time, I thought I had really hit the nail on the head. A few years later, after working to solve problems for citizens who needed help, I realized how different government functioned and what its role really was. Government could always work to be more efficient – but not at the expense of providing essential services to Florida's citizens. But enough regrets about mouthing-off before I knew what I was talking about. I had in front of me what would turn out to become my life's greatest challenge – to put a newly formed State Agency on the right path.

Facing a Culture of No

The legislature had established a NEW Agency - the Department of Management Services (DMS). In fact, what they had actually done was merge two highly regulatory and bureaucratic departments. Together, they provided the internal infrastructure and support services required for State Agencies to fulfill their mission. The DMS was mandated by the legislature to become more efficient, cutting costs by 10%, and also to be more effective, becoming a real resource to its customers — State Agencies. My goal was to find a way for DMS to say yes – not always to begin with no and then, with a lot of prodding, reluctantly shift to maybe.

I had taken to heart the lessons learned from David Osborne's *Reinventing Government* (required reading in the Governor's office). I was on a mission. I wanted to make government work better and cost less while still putting the well-being of our citizens first.

I knew if I was going to make progress reinventing government, I had to begin with the culture, to get the new Department of Management Services to start seeing SERVICES in all caps.

DEPARTMENT OF MANAGEMENT

SERVICES

The Agency had to gain the trust of its customers – other State Agencies. To do that, the employees of DMS had to not only talk about being a Resource, they actually had to *be* a Resource. The culture would need to change and I would need to sustain my positive attitude, continually communicating the vision at regularly scheduled All Staff meetings.

The new DMS graphics shop created the Agency Logo, designed to send the message that SERVICES were central to their mission.

My intention was to move ahead at a steady pace making sure they didn't run the clock out on me. But just in case, I had my disruptive mode ready in the wings. Some thought my 3rd World Country Takeover Strategy was a little draconian. But to Reinvent DMS, major disruption could be necessary. For me, failure was not an option. It wasn't likely the Agency's employees would read the newsletter and buy what I was selling. It would take more than talk to change the culture.

Some who were way down the org chart, were open to change. But their boss and their boss's boss would hold them back and even inflict punishment if they got out of line. They would hear; "He's gonna cut your job, and what does this new, so-called Secretary know? Why should we change what's working?" If I was going to build support from the ground up, it was important to appear reasonable, to be as persuasive as possible without mandates. But if the *rope-a-dope* delaying tactics persisted, force would likely be needed, at least to kick-start the process. I knew my time was limited, 4 to 6 years was all I had, and they were career government employees. They could just play along and wait me out.

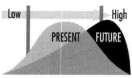

To Reinvent the Agency, it would be necessary for its employees to become a High Performance Workforce.

I like to think it would have been possible to gain the employees' confidence and get buy-in for my ideas with a new brand focused on Service, internal publications to tout their

"Never confuse motion with action."

Ben Franklin

success, and face-to-face meetings to listen to their concerns and share my plans. I even had hoped they would see being more productive would equate to better job security. But as I reflected on the comments of the Deputy Secretary on my first day, I knew the internal resistance would be almost insurmountable and my

3rd World Country Takeover Strategy might be necessary.

The Takeover Strategy, designed to expedite large scale change, had 4 phases: First Seize communications; next,

Take over the Banks; then stage Public Executions; and finally Rewrite the Constitution. In the end, the "takeover strategy" was necessary to implement the change agenda.

Phase I – Seize Communications

The new Agency, DMS, now had 10 Divisions. Each worked like an independent organization governed by what they saw as their special rules. This redundant structure needed to change and I would start with the Divisional newsletters. Can you believe DMS also published 10 Newsletters? To control the message I abolished all 10 and launched a single Departmental Newsletter. Each division was asked to contribute articles to the newly established Communication office. The Communications Director, someone I had worked closely with and trusted implicitly, would select what would be included. We thought about a quarterly publication but decided more was better, at least to start, and went with monthly. As you would expect, this didn't go over with the Division leaders who had used the Newsletter as a way to put out their divisions' propaganda.

The unified publication was the first step in breaking down the stove-pipe structure and beginning to build a shared vision.

Phase II – Take over the Banks

To get people onboard, they had to know where you wanted to go and be able to see themselves going there. The Department News Letter was a good first step. But without control of the money flow, you have nothing behind the rhetoric. I found a candidate for a new Finance Director who understood I was making the decisions on where to invest and where to cut. Unfortunately, the position currently reported to my old nemesis, the obviously disloyal DGS Deputy Secretary for Administration who was still hanging on. I let the current

Finance Director go and filled the position with my candidate, having him report directly to me. It took less than a month to get control of our budget and begin to realign spending with my priorities. With his loss of financial control, the disloyal Deputy Secretary problem would resolve itself.

Phase III – Public Executions

The old regime Deputy was the first to go. Fortunately, I didn't need to fire him – he resigned and found a position at another Agency. Most knew he was on the outs with me but his decision to leave was a signal to some members of the old guard that they better adapt to the new world order or leave. The next senior staff person who had been an obstructionist from the beginning was the General Counsel.

The General Counsel was always able to find a statute that I would violate if I did what I saw as ". . . in the best interest of the people of Florida". This was my first top management fire. I told her face to face it wasn't personal, but our priorities were different. I gave her a generous payout of 90 days and a good letter of recommendation. She left quietly.

I brought in a well-respected lawyer who lived out of town at the time but had previously been in Tallahassee serving as General Counsel for the Department of Revenue. He was a top-notch pro with experience in government who could not be accused as being a crony. I knew this hire would be suspect if I didn't get someone with impeccable credentials. He came in to talk about my expectations. I explained my theory of how Newton's Law applied to the statutes – For every statue there's an equal and opposite statute. He got it (even though he was pretty sure that was not what Newton meant). The chemistry was good and I sensed he really did understand my statute theory. I hired him and quickly began to see he had a gift, he was a master at applying "or in the

47

best interest of the State of Florida" to any initiative I believed was good for the taxpayers.

I had also identified two division directors who had never got on board and were still hoping to turn the clock back. I found one director another job at an Agency where he was seen as an asset; the other took early retirement. As this purging process unfolded, I had one other Division director who had only paid lip service to my initiatives. I went to his office to lay it on the line. He thought he was a goner.

We had a frank conversation, mostly me laying down the law and him nodding yes. He said, with some conviction, he saw the light. I'm guessing he moved from advisory to advocate to avoid the guillotine. Despite my suspicion of his miraculous conversion, he became a positive force in the Agency for the rest of my tenure.

Phase IV – Rewrite the Constitution

Whenever there is a change in leadership, especially in government, you'll hear "This guy won't last long; we'll just wait him out." They had a point about me not becoming a permanent fixture, but I was intent on making my changes stick, not being wiped out the minute I left. In the case of government, changing the statutes is the equivalent of rewriting the constitution. Statutes are the means to institutionalize

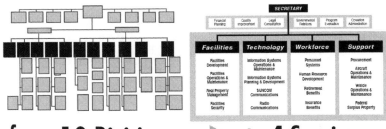

from **10** Divisions ➡ to **4** Services

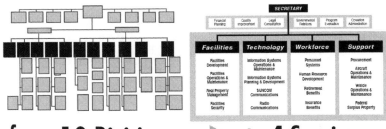

change. For example, if you want to reduce your Agency Divisions from 10 to 4 you'll need to put that in statute. It took me five legislative sessions, but I got that done. The Takeover Strategy was effective as shock therapy but to sustain change, to make it stick, that would take constant pressure. It was time to roll up my sleeves and do the hard work needed to move us from **Regulator to Resource**.

11 SUSTAINABLE CHANGE STARTS WITH THE CULTURE

Regulator to Resource <15 was a big idea, it required changing people's attitude at the enterprise level. I had begun the change process; put together a lot of promotional materials – the Works Better and Cost Less stuff – and made Regulator to Resource the centerpiece of the Departmental Newsletter.

TakeAway <15

A slogan can build your brand

One part of your communication strategy is to express your idea in three to five words that capture people's imagination. Don't discount a well turned phrase.

I had also let all 2,000 employees hear directly from me, face to face. I felt it

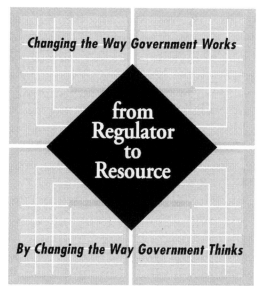

Changing the Way Government Works

from
Regulator
to
Resource

By Changing the Way Government Thinks

was important for them to hear my ideas, but I also wanted to get their input.

Before I scheduled the meeting, I put out a request for reactions to the top 3 initiatives I planned to implement and a space to ask whatever they wanted. The responses would be anonymous. I got 400 responses. Not bad.

Of the 3 initiatives, 200 leaned one way, 200 the other. "I really admire your commitment to improving our services" or "I don't get it – the services we are providing are top notch, NO CHANGES NECESSARY." So how did this help me? It didn't.

Of those who had a personal question, the number-one issue was pay – they wanted more. Who woulda' thought. No one suggested what I had hoped to hear – tying pay to performance.

At this point, I was getting discouraged.**<16** How was I going to build consensus? I came to realize I needed to rethink how I would go through what lawyers call the Discovery Phase. It was the last time I would rely on polling or focus groups to guide my thinking. I became a Steve Jobs disciple who said *"They'll know what they want when I show them what they want."* I think Jobs was the king of Audaciousness.

"You can't just ask customers what they want and then try to give that to them. By the time you get it built, they'll want something new."

Steve Jobs

I decided I could get my message across best, if I had an example of what I was after. A good slogan wouldn't be enough. I wanted my internal audience to say "Oh, now I get it." But I also wanted my customers, State Agencies, to notice our new attitude –

"Well done is better than well said."

Ben Franklin

We Were a RESOURCE.

I needed to consider an example that would impact the Agency directly and as soon as possible. Also I wanted an example that other Agencies could visualize applying to their situation. <17 State Purchasing offered a good test case. Purchasing was a process that touched all our Agency customers.

TakeAway <17

Teach by Example

Providing an example of your innovative idea, especially one that can be replicated, will increase your potential of success.

Look for ways to demonstrate how the innovative change will have positive results.

Remember, my Department was the internal service agency. Our mission was to help Agencies provide their services to citizens as efficiently as possible. (In fact, after I left State government, DMS came up with a slogan which really captured the Agency's goal as I saw it: *We serve those who serve Florida*). In addition to Purchasing having a broad impact on our customers, the Division Director was committed to my goal – making DMS a RESOURCE .

I had heard that the Department of Transportation (DOT) was having difficulty getting the Tire contract completed. This was a very big deal to DOT and they were fed-up with the DMS purchasing contract manager assigned to the Tire contract. Buying Tires, what could be more basic? I decided this would be a good chance for DMS to turn things around.

I got the impression this was about showing the DOT who was in charge – and it wasn't them. It was a cultural thing and I was going to intervene.

I called the DOT Secretary and asked if I could try something to expedite getting the contract executed. I outlined the idea and he said let's give it a shot. First I would OutPost one the Purchasing managers to the DOT building to work there once a week. This would give both sides a chance to work together face to face, not just their side submitting a request and waiting 2 weeks for our side to send a rejection form. Being co-located, the DOT staff could lay out their issues in detail and get our contract manager's response on the spot, maybe each not thinking like "sides," but more like process partners. Everyone knew the DOT staff had forgotten more about tires than we would ever know. I then told the Purchasing Director that I would expect a call from the Secretary of DOT that would thank me for solving the problem and treating them as valued customers. I gave him 30 days. <18

I got the call I was looking for from the DOT Secretary 3 weeks later. Mission accomplished. The success of Purchasing's OutPosting initiative caught fire and the Director of Purchasing imple-

TakeAway <18

Use data to substantiate your success

Don't start making changes without a measurement strategy. You won't be able to sustain change unless you can produce evidence of progress. Develop a cost/benefit analysis that supports your efforts. Solicit testimonials from participants and clients. Then promote your accomplishments internally and externally.

mented it in several other Agencies. The DMS communication's office put the story on the front page of the newsletter supported with quotes from the DOT staff. It was important to do some internal marketing to get our team fired up. And I knew there was nothing more important to foster success than to have success. It would be contagious.

I had put a dent in changing attitudes. Now I turned my attention to changing the process. We would begin by focusing on tracking time, what was getting done during the time spent doing it. I had the IT team program a tool that would automate the collection process – the Time Accountable System (TAS). The hard- copy time card would be terminated, replaced by the on-line TAS, designed to analyze data in order to measure productivity. Tracking time was critical but we needed to build a spirit of teamwork, a Shared Risk, Shared Reward approach.

13 IMPLEMENTING A DISRUPTIVE PROCESS

TakeAway <19

Tie your vision to clear methods of implementation

You must clearly define the way people will participate. People won't jump overboard, you need to put them in a life boat. You'll need specific programs with defined responsibilities structured to support your vision.

CPR – the Change Management tool

To tie accountability to accomplishment, the agency launched their stovepipe busting initiative - CPR for DMS.<19

The idea was to identify people from   different Divisions with complementary skills, have them work as teams on Projects producing measurable Results, what I called the Cross-functional, Project driven, Results oriented initiative.

CPR disrupted the existing chain of command despite management's organized resistance. It turned out people of diverse talents – a lawyer, an accountant, an insurance expert, and someone

53

from the maintenance staff — worked together as a team to solve a specific problem. CPR was picking up steam but it needed to be supercharged. I needed to link performance to reward. I created a new program – Incentives for Success. It would provide both recognition and financial reward for team success. In 6 months, CPR became the work mode of choice.

Projects are the operational elements of the Strategic Plan – a way to pull groups of talented people together for a limited time to improve quality or reduce costs

All the big vision stuff and motivational hype was nothing when compared to **CPR coupled with our Incentive program**. It was a game-changer, a practical approach to implement the goals of the agencies' strategic plan. More importantly, **CPR** was *a stove-pipe buster.*

C P R

Project Starter Kit

Office of Quality Improvement

The Agency was making progress in moving from a Regulator to a Resource, I was seeing the culture begin to change, but I needed to recharge my batteries, to take my foot off the gas and see things from a distance. I got an invitation to participate in a learning opportunity I couldn't pass up.

The Project Starter Kit was published by the Quality Improvement Office and acted as a printed "how to" manual for employees.

I left Tallahassee for Boston. I was going to attend a 10-day Harvard Business School workshop for Government Leaders. Much was memorable. I had a chance to get a tour of the School of Architecture that had been arranged by a friend, a Sarasota Architect who taught there during summer sessions. That brought back memories of my days as a student in the Design Studio when anything was possible. But the experience that I remember to this day is a case study shared in class.

The following is my best recollection, with some added research and embellishment of the case study presented. I've titled the case The Gun that Won the West.

14 UNINTENDED RESULTS - WRONG TIME, WRONG USER

The Gun that Won the West

Shots rang out on the Whitehouse lawn. It was 1863, the Civil War had been raging for two years and shooting was not allowed in Washington, especially near the President's home. People rushed to the scene to find President Lincoln with a rifle in his hand.

The President was conducting a hands-on test of a technological innovation, a new type of rifle that could give his troops an advantage on the field of battle.

An entrepreneur, Oliver Winchester, who was standing next to the President pitching his product, had recently offered the lever-action, rapid-fire rifle to the Union's Ordnance Department.

The head of the Ordinance Department, General James Ripley, was known for his unyielding adherence to the rules.[<20] He saw his job was to increase the North's output of working, easy-to-use, standardized, Springfield muskets for use by the hundreds of thousands of troops in the field.

For Ripley, this experimental weapon was of no interest. He told Winchester his rifle was useless, despite its "singular beauty and ingenious design."

He saw the weapon as underpowered, would waste ammunition, and couldn't be manufactured in sufficient volume.

The President, who had many serious matters to attend to, had directed Ripley to contract with Winchester, assuming his order would be executed. But Ripley tied up the process in bureaucratic purchasing procedures. He was following the President's orders, but had no intention of ever buying guns from Winchester.

Unfortunately, the Union troops never got to benefit from Winchester's innovation. Ripley was able to stall until the end of the war, keeping his supply chain process intact and his muzzle-loading muskets in production.

At the end of the war, when Vice President Johnson assumed power, the experiment with Winchester's innovative rifle was

TakeAway <20

Cracking the status quo may require you to walk in your resistor's shoes

Try to see it from the Resistor's perspective. Listen to the naysayers and determine "what's in it for them." Drill down and re-examine the innovation's challenges from the stakeholders' perspectives.

Accept reasonable criticisms and, when possible, adjust your initiative to address the concerns.

declared impractical and the Ordnance Department went back to business as usual.

But the Winchester rifle was not destined to die an early death. A decade later, this innovation was ready for center stage being heralded as "the gun that won the west."

An unexpected outcome

During his Civil War service, General George Custer test-fired the Winchester. He immediately recognized the strategic advantage it could provide his cavalry. But ten years later Custer was still unable to procure the Winchesters for his army, now fighting in the west.

The Plains Indians, who would join the battle at Little Big Horn, had also seen the rifle's strategic advantage but were not subject to the U.S. army's procurement process. They had traded for a significant supply of rapid-fire rifles to arm their Braves.

On June 26,1876, still without repeater rifles, Custer and his troops were sent to their graves.   THE END

This is one of my favorite stories. It has many lessons an innovator should learn.

1. **Have a Good idea** – The Innovator has a revolutionary innovation that results in an incredibly valuable outcome – it can save lives.

2. **Have support from Leadership** - The Innovator has the backing of a high-level decision-maker. In this case, the President of the United States.

"Sometimes life's going to hit you in the head with a brick. Don't lose faith. I'm convinced that the only thing that kept me going was that I loved what I did."

Steve Jobs

3. **Be ready for the Resistance** – The mid-level management was "the expert" and is more than satisfied with their process and results. The manager in charge was responsible for delivering a large volume of product (guns and ammunition) that worked 100% of the time. <21

4. **Know when the Timing is right** – The innovation was ahead of its time. It took a decade to finally become recognized for its importance.

5. **Expect the unexpected** – It was used for its intended function but not, in all cases, by its target market. In this instance, the lives saved were Native Americans, not US Army soldiers. <22 This is a point I have been obsessed with lately. As an innovator with the intention of making a positive contribution, a word of caution – your grand idea, in the wrong hands, can be weaponized for a purpose not of their own.

Going to Harvard, if only for ten days, was a great break from the Reinventing Government ground war. It helped me to see that others from around the country were faced with the same challenges. I realized the situation in Florida was not unique, I felt like part of a national movement along with my fellow insurgents.

TakeAway <21

Resistance to change will test your confidence

You're likely to face strong resistance, but keep your enthusiasm up. Be persistent, maintain your passion, don't lose faith in your idea.

TakeAway <22

How you intended things to go is not always what happens

Your innovative idea may ultimately be considered a success but not in the way you had envisioned. Watch for changes in circumstances that can cast a new light on your initiative, redirecting your goals.

EPILOGUE

Oliver Winchester was a manufacturer and a marketing guy. He knew how to structure deals, get venture capital, set up and take over companies. These are valuable skills, but a pivotal player to the Winchester rifle's ultimate success was a company engineer's innovation. Although Winchester was persistent, to him, the repeater rifle was just another product to market. He was not as much a purebred innovator with a passion for his idea.

Although Winchester had a functioning model and had produced around 14,000 rifles before the end of the war, to be honest, the technology was not refined and his manufacturing process couldn't be ramped up for mass production. Ripley needed hundreds of thousands of rifles and they had to work without fail under battle conditions. Winchester's product also wasn't 100% reliable. At the time, Ripley was right on the substance but wrong for not getting his department positioned for the future innovation.

TakeAway <23

Don't assume top level support will ensure success

It's always valuable to have the top person on board. But most initiatives are killed by midlevel management.

Try to get support at every level of the chain of command.

Winchester had a powerful advocate – the President. But Lincoln had his hands full and only had time to direct Ripley to contract with Winchester. The President was not able to ensure his orders were carried out. <23

Ripley had no respect for the President's expertise in determining what type of arms the troops needed. He saw himself as the sole decision-maker and although he recognized the beauty of the Winchester rifle, his supply chain was working and he was totally committed to the rifles he was supplying. Ripley was not going to change. Several years after the Civil War, the Winchester finally met with success and was dubbed "the gun that won the west."

After my Fact Finding trip to Harvard it was time to get back to work. I had made some progress changing the DMS culture, implementing my Regulator to Resource vision. But I was soon going to be exposed to a new technology that would revolutionize my approach to Reinventing Government.

15 RECOGNIZE A SEISMIC TECHNOLOGY SHIFT

"I am terribly fascinated with things that I don't understand."
Richard Saul Wurman

I can say without qualification that the most important revelation of my lifetime came to me from a young woman who visited my office the first day I was back from Boston. A vendor had gotten 20 minutes on my calendar to pitch her service – an online training program. Online? What was that, I wondered? She opened up her laptop, which was more of a novelty in 1993, and proceeded to bring up her presentation. She said it was running in a browser.

To me, it looked like a typical Power-Point presentation. What the hell was a browser? I said I was not familiar with the Mosaic software (forerunner to NetScape). For the next 10 minutes I got educated. She was accessing her presentation on a server in Minnesota. She was on a network, the internet. I said I was interested in her training courses but the fact was, all I could

TakeAway <24
Things can change in the blink of an eye

Sometimes you get wrapped up in the day to day work and miss something that is revolutionary.

Sometimes it's not what it is but what it could be. Keep your eyes and mind open.

think about was her remotely accessing her presentation.

In that 20 minutes I had learned just enough to be dangerous. I couldn't figure out specifically what steps I needed to take but I was sure this internet thing was going to be important. **<24** I had no idea. Technology was going to take a big Leap and redefine everything, including how government worked.

16 AN ATTACK CAN BE CATALYTIC

My days were overscheduled; there were lots of pressing issues and I put the internet in the *"I'll get to that soon"* category. Then, some 3 months later, my priorities changed. State Government was the target of a scathing article published in a prominent statewide magazine.

The headline – **"The Digital Deficit."**

One *pull-quote* said "If most of the information superhighway bypasses Florida, the state's economic development may be stunted."

As expected, I got a call from the Governor. "Hey, I thought you were the tech guru – why are we behind?"**<25** I responded calmly, "I'm on it; give me a few days to verify the facts and I'll report back." The truth was, all I knew was what the online training vendor had shown me a few months ago. And I had no idea what I would report back. I needed to get the facts and a plan of action – Fast.

TakeAway <25

A threatening challenge can lead to a dramatic innovation

Some change is a result of a slow evolutionary process. But an attack can create a sense of urgency generating a rapid response.

Be ready to think fast, improvise if necessary and accommodate changes as you go.

17 DO YOUR HOMEWORK

Doing the research was something this Governor was familiar with. I remember the then Senator Chiles sharing a tale of his visit to the *U.S.S. Forrestal*, an aircraft carrier cruising the Mediterranean. A small group of us were having lunch at his son's restaurant, the Sand Bar on Anna Maria Island. His recounting sounded like quite an adventure. As he wrapped it up I said "Sounds like a junket to me." No one said a word. Oops. He turned to me and gave me his patented stare. He glared for so long that I got very uncomfortable and then proclaimed *"Son, it was a Fact-Finding mission."* Lucky for me, the lunch group all laughed. I hoped it was what he said but more likely they were laughing at how stupid I was. Obviously, I had a *political-speak* deficit. Now it was time for me to go on a *Fact-Finding mission* of my own.

Silicon Valley

Washington D.C.

North Carolina

A "Fact Finding" mission
to assess the state of the
Information Super Highway

Florida

I knew, despite the criticism, that the then Senator Al Gore had offered the legislation that created ARPANET, the initiative that provided the foundation for the Internet. The Governor had contacts with his office and our staff arranged a meeting. The article that trashed Florida highlighted the accomplishments in North Carolina and touted them as a leader in utilizing the Superhighway. We got on their IT leader's schedule for a briefing. Then, I knew I had to see what was going on in Silicon Valley, the center of technology innovation. After a little digging I found the guy who had written the code for Mosaic while still in college. He was launching a company to offer a commercial version of the browser – Netscape 1.0. I called, said I represented the State of Florida and was interested in putting the Netscape browser on our State Term Contract. That did it. Marc Andreessen, the co-founder of the company, agreed to meet.

I went first to Washington to meet with Gore's people, then to N.C. to see how a statewide broadband network worked, and finally California – the land of OZ.

WOW! What a tour. My week on the road, Fact-Finding, was over. My head was spinning, filled with ideas. I had met with the thought leaders that were going to change the world and I now understood why Florida had to Leap into the fuzzy future as quickly as possible. It was too early to predict the final destination but we had to start the journey. On the Red-eye from Silicon Valley heading back to Tallahassee I didn't sleep. It was all the time I would have to envision a plan, or at the least come up with my new elevator pitch for our counterattack. The Governor needed to announce his actions aimed to

TakeAway <26

Form a SkunkWorks to kick-start your idea

The Steve Jobs Mac team is a good skunkworks example. If your challenge is to re-invent a large organization, put a "strike force" of people in place that are 100% committed to implementing your vision.

Jobs said "I'd rather be a Pirate than join the Navy." You can innovate in a large institution where conforming to rules is required, but you need to find a way to work outside the inside system.

dispel the fallout from the Digital Deficit article.

I got to the office early the next morning and gathered up the key people that would form the initiative's SkunkWorks.**<26** I pronounced with authority, "We're gonna put Florida on the Information Highway." The response – blank stares. No wonder, I had no idea what that really meant or how to do it. But I did know why – the race to connect everyone to everything was going to change the world, and Florida had to be a player.

I shared the knowledge I had gained while on my Fact-Finding mission. Verbalizing what I had learned helped me to move out of the fog and begin to see the possibilities. I started to see this application of technology could, from a macro perspective, change the relationship of Government with its Citizens. From a more practical point of view, it could streamline access to services and improve delivery, making Government work better and cost less. I'm not sure it was the silver bullet to changing the way Government works, but I was starting to believe it was pretty close.**<27**

I briefed the Governor on what I had seen and laid out what DMS had begun working on. I said I would be ready to present a more detailed plan in about two weeks. The pressure was on for him to clear our name so he went public with an announcement. His Secretary of

TakeAway <27
Timing is everything

You need to make sure conditions are right for your innovation to work. Starting with a great idea that will produce something customers want is key. But also authority, money, technology, an efficient process need to be in balance – coming together when all conditions are "right."

And don't forget, time marches on. What was ripe in the Summer will be rotten in the Fall.

Management Services had met with key Technology leaders from around the country and had his team working on a plan to address Florida's Digital Deficit. He told the press he expected to have an announcement in two weeks. So, as if there wasn't enough pressure, the alarm was set and the clock was ticking.

Before getting started I wanted to share what I had learned on my trip with Rhea. She was my best sounding-board when I was at 50,000 ft. where the air is thin. I dropped by the Mansion after dinner and we sat in the sunroom.

I brought the magazine article that was titled "Florida's Digital Deficit." Rhea had gotten an earful from Lawton so she had an idea of what I was up against. I gave her the highlights of the trip, especially what I learned in California. I told her about my newly formed SkunkWorks, and my vision for what this Digital Revolution meant for Florida. Hard for me to imagine, but for just a few seconds, she was speechless. She knew this was our next Leap together – it was Dream Home 2.0. She asked if I would bring my skunkworks team over for lunch tomorrow. Of course, I'd love the chance to have her creative energy in the mix and I was sure it would super-charge the team. She was right, this was the next Leap – but the scale and scope was beyond our wildest imagination.

18 DON'T OVERTHINK – FOLLOW YOUR INSTINCTS

With the Governor's authority and the First Ladies enthusiastic support, the adventure began. Two weeks went by and no one was clamoring for the Governor's announcement. I just kept my head down and kept pushing. In 30 days we had made visible progress. We had Netscape 1.0 on State Term Contract at $50 per copy. I'm not joking – in the early days, you had to buy each copy of the browser software. I bought a thousand copies, one for every desktop in my Agency. It cost $50,000. Worth every penny. We had the servers configured to host our homepage and the server room set to go, mainly because DMS had control of the State's Data Center and the staff worked for us. And besides, this was cutting-edge stuff and the techies loved to experiment. <28

We had executed a contract with our private sector Telecommunications service provider to connect our servers to the information highway. There were a few *ahead of their time* HTML coders from our Information Services Division. They would code our webpage prototype. The graphics team was working on logos and the look and flow of the website. Our print designers were fast becoming digital designers. We were gaining momentum. It was starting to become real.

TakeAway <28

Having the latitude to experiment is essential for early adopters

Innovators, by nature, are early adopters and anything that hasn't been mainstreamed will be risky. Being early means you'll need the opportunity to make a few mistakes, to explore options, some that don't pan out. Make sure you have been given the authority, or are audacious enough to take it, so you can experiment and survive a few failures.

19 DECLARE VICTORY, BUT KEEP RUNNING HARD

A Cracker-Style Rollout

We scheduled a press conference for the Governor to make the announcement – Florida was off the dirt road, as had been alluded to in the nasty article, and now driving on the Information Highway.

Everyone knew Lawton wasn't much on technology. I needed a way for him to get engaged and send the message that Florida had overcome its Digital Deficit. I thought of a hook that would appeal to a Florida Cracker (this was not a dig – It's a way of saying he was a down-to-earth man of the people).

We located a pecan farm that was about 50 miles out of town and on-line. The owner's son worked at the University's Super Computer Research Institute and had built a website for the family Pecan business. We contacted the owner who was, like our Governor, a proud **Florida Cracker***. He agreed to personally deliver a 10 pound bag of pecans to the press room on cue. The press was assembled and the Governor made his formal announcement – Florida was now on the Information Highway. We then got him to simulate using the computer and clicking a few keys to order a bag of pecans.

* Florida Cracker

The tern today is used with great pride by those like Lawton Chiles whose families have lived in Florida for many generations, descendants of "frontier people" who flourished before air conditioning, paved roads and the overly restrictive rules imposed by the government bureaucracy.

The Governor proclaims Florida is on the "Information Highway."

Three seconds later our pecan farmer came through the side door with the bag of pecans over his shoulder (you know, the ones Lawton just ordered over the internet) and presented them to the Governor. It was a big hit and the perfect photo-op. Lawton let out with a big belly laugh. And he kept the pecans.

The State's first Homepage was focused on connecting communities with government services. It went through several versions but would be refocused and renamed Government Services Direct.

20 SECURE RECOGNITION AS THE NATIONAL LEADER

Over the next year, the initiative to put Florida online touched almost every employee at DMS. Everyone was experimenting, discovering the power of being connected using their desktop computer. The DMS team didn't just hear about the internet, they got to experience it. Many were baffled, but the early adopters lead the way and soon people that were turned off, were turned on.

They began to understand how this power of connection would shape the gathering of information, expedite transactions, and allow people to work collaboratively.

The wild enthusiasm was contagious. DMS was leading the way for other Agencies to computerize their processes. This initiative, as much as anything we had done so far, was making other Agencies see DMS as a Resource. We became their Tech consultants. This is an important lesson, if you want people to believe you, know what you're talking about,

TakeAway <29

Do it first, then share it

It's harder to sell it if you haven't done it or don't use it. There is no substitute for first-hand experience. Confidence in your idea will spread if you leverage the lessons of experience and share it with others.

Do it First, Then Share it. <29

The Digital Deficit was a thing of the past. Florida was not just in the information age race, it had climbed to the top.

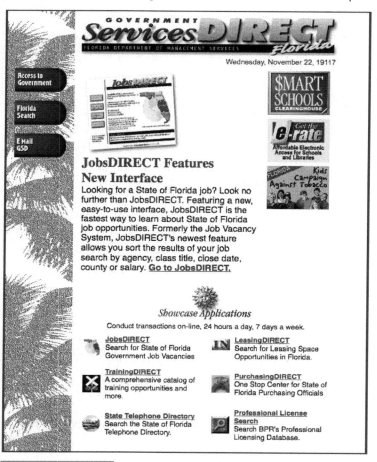

It was selected two years running as the best Government website in the Nation and Bill Gates, speaking at the national Governors Association, used Florida as an example of a Government website that was changing the way Government worked.

I was lucky enough to be in attendance at the Governors meeting and proud to hear what Gates said, but even more thrilled to see the crowd that gathered around Lawton, quizzing him on how he had done it. This was a memorable day, I couldn't wait to share it with Rhea and the development team.

The Gates presentation helped to validate what we were doing. There's no better compliment than having an industry leader recognize your work in front of your peers. But there's more. He also gave Florida another nod of approval by featuring us in his book – *Business @ the Speed of Thought: Using the Digital Nervous System.* **<30** I was quoted as he opened the chapter on Government – Take Government to the People – "*We must empower citizens to act for themselves without having to go through a bureaucracy. Government agencies have to think of themselves as a resource and not as an office of regulation. And guess what? It's fun to help citizens solve their problems.*"

Government Services Direct was getting acclaim but it was more importantly, earning it's name – **DIRECT**. Every new application was making government more efficient. One app that had a big impact on cutting the cost of government was **Leasing DIRECT**. In simple terms, it was an "*electronic Dating Service*", matching Agencies who needed rental space with private sector building owners looking for good tenants.

This model of matching buyers with sellers is at the heart of many of today's successful online businesses.

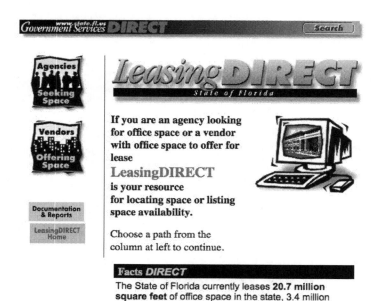

Facts **DIRECT**

The State of Florida currently leases **20.7 million square feet** of office space in the state, 3.4 million square feet in the Tallahassee area alone.

Leasing DIRECT established a set of quality standards that space for lease was required to meet. Once reviewed and approved by DMS, the property owners could add their available space and terms to the Leasing Direct database.

Then, Agencies could enter in their needs and find a match. This gave Agencies more control, allowing them to move more quickly. DMS was cutting red tape and fulfilling it's mission – to be a Resource. The process was more efficient, but there was an even bigger benefit to the taxpayers – Cutting Cost.

In the first year, many existing leases were renegotiated and new leases were executed at a much lower rate. So why did annual lease costs drop by $12,000,000. **Competition**! It was simple. With quality set by agreed upon standards, the key variable was price. The Agencies search results were sorted by price with the lowest at the top. Being good public servants, they would select the best price. The trick was, on the 1st of every month, building owners could adjust their price to meet or beat the competition. This Direct application is a great example of how this use of technology helped to tap the power of the free market.

Another DIRECT app had a different benefit – it opened the job market, allowing Agencies access to a larger talent pool.

State of Florida

On-Line Job Application

Job Application Download PDF

Employment Guide

Frequently Asked Questions

JobsDIRECT is your resource for locating government job opportunities in Florida.

Choose a region at right to locate a government job vacancy in that region, or choose one of these options:

- **Statewide**
- **Out of State**
- **Out of Country**

Find out the number of current job advertisements by agency. Check out other useful areas in the left column including: the State of Florida Job Application (PDF Version), and the On-Line Job Application.

For more information about JobsDIRECT, please contact the JobsMaster.

Find out which counties are in each region.

Facts DIRECT

In 1997, the State of Florida has hired over 1,000 people who submitted their applications using the On-line Job Application.

The great majority of applicants for jobs in the state capital where Agencies are headquartered, come from two sources; people you know and proximity – someone who lives in the capital region. But **Jobs DIRECT** would change that.

Once up and running with our online application and inter-view scheduling system in place, the State began to get job seekers from not only all over Florida but from around the world. And we were getting a lot more diversity which was something the Governor encouraged. One case in point stands out.

We were advertising the Deputy Director position within the DMS Capital Police Division. Both by tradition and experi-ence this was a very homogeneous unit. **Jobs DIRECT** dramatically increased the applicant pool. We found an extremely qualified candidate working in Miami/Dade county as an assistant chief of police. Her interview was stellar. She received and accepted the Division's job offer. We now had our first woman Deputy Director of Capital Police.

Jobs Direct completely reshaped the landscape, infusing new talent into government service.

Our tech team was in high gear, cranking out more DIRECT applications – Purchasing DIRECT, HR DIRECT and Training DIRECT. Each addressed an important need for government to improve the services being offered. And some, like **Leasing DIRECT** generated a funding stream to support new applica-tion development as well as keeping the apps current.

Of the 10 Divisions housed within DMS, The Division of Communications had left a mark with *Government Services Direct*. Florida was now a National IT leader and the Division had played an important role.

But another one of the DMS Divisions also had a *claim to fame* in the Tech space. The Department's Division of Building Construction introduced what it called the *Distributive Collabo-rative Network (DCN)*.

The following are excerpts from the Divisions webpage.

New ways to improve efficiency

In an effort to overcome project delays, the Division of Building Construction has launched a new project called the Distributive Collaborative Network (DCN). DCN is a high speed telecommunications system used by the Division of Building Construction to link its regional offices with the main office in Tallahassee. The project was begun in the Fall of 1996 and the network was in place and operational by February 1997. Documents which previously took days to transfer can now be delivered in a matter of minutes.

There's More To Come

the network is in place and operational, but there is still more to be done. DCN is currently in its test phase. By the time DCN is fully implemented, all new projects managed by DBC will be included, and all project design and scheduling information will be incorporated. Architects as far away a Miami will be able to send drawings over telephone lines in a matter of minutes. Furthermore, design drawings and progress reports will be available to Florida's Citizens over the Florida Communities Network. The result - fewer project delays, financial savings and better service to the people of Florida.

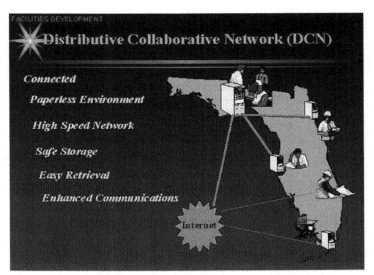

NOTE: Some webpages were posted before the *DMS Graphic Police* had a chance to work their magic. But, on the bright side, Departments were taking initiative, becoming a Resource, finding ways to make the agency "work better and cost less".

In addition to the Tech initiative, the Division was also gaining national recognition beyond the virtual space.

21 MAKING THE WORKPLACE A PRODUCTIVITY TOOL

Writing off 1 million to save 10

TakeAway <31

Weigh the value of scrapping one approach for another

If you join an initiative that's underway and you recognize the direction will not result in the best outcome, you must speak up. But be ready with why the initiative must be redirected. You'll need some rational arguments – the long term cost will be much lower or a key factor was not considered. Don't yell STOP until you have an argument that will justify the need to change directions.

As if the internet revolution wasn't enough excitement, DMS was launching a new Government Office Park in Tallahassee. It had gone through the planning stage under the authority of DGS – now a part of DMS. In fact, at the time of the merger, DGS had spent almost a million dollars for architectural and engineering drawings. Their vision was every Agency that located in the park would contract for a "custom" building to fit their "special" needs. I was less than enthusiastic. In fact, I saw this approach as a waste of both time and money. **<31**

I was not sold on the idea that the work of each Agency was substantially different than the next. State Agencies, particularly with the information age in full swing, were communicating with each other and directly with citizens to provide services and enforce regulations when necessary. In general, the work flow was similar so I believed the building accommodations could be similar. Similar, or what is termed Prototype buildings would have two important benefits.

75

First the cost of the construction documents would be reduced by only being charged a *Reuse Fee* when the buildings were replicated. Also, with standard buildings, the Maintenance cost would be lower. But I was concerned if I ditched the plans that cost a million dollars my detractors would use it to bring me down. I needed some data to backup taking action.

Looking long term and seeing the "people cost" (Occupants' Payroll) as the major expense was the key innovative insight, defining the initiative as the High Performance Workplace.

I had my numbers guy do a 10-year projection. His calculations supported making the change. The savings from going with Prototypes, abandoning the custom approach, would save a little over 10 million dollars. The maintenance savings was harder to estimate but the Facilities team guessed about $200,000 a year. The decision was still likely to draw criticism but I was confident the benefits outweighed the risk. I gathered my supporting materials and pulled the trigger. In addition to the time and money savings, I also wanted to put forward a more high level argument for starting fresh with a new criteria for the Architects to consider – occupant productivity.

This chart depicts a broader view that includes the building's initial construction cost, the 30 year operational costs, and the payroll costs of the occupants.

Workplace & the High Performance Organization

Much of what was driving my Reinventing Government mission was tied to Performance. I wanted the new complex to be efficient by the traditional measures: energy consumption and a winning net-to-gross ratio (that simply means you get the most usable square footage possible). But if you look at cost over the life of the buildings, **<32** People are your most expensive

TakeAway <32

Consider your initiatives Life Cycle Cost

If you're offering a product, you'll need to factor in how long it will be useful. Products with a long life can afford a bigger up-front investment in time and money. Short Life Cycles are the opposite – you need to get in and get out. But being able to plan for a big return or large cumulative savings in the distant future is difficult to sell unless you are designing some-thing to last for 100 years (e.g. the Hoover Dam).

cost. I wanted to introduce that concept, to make Workplace part of delivering the High Performance Organization.

The feedback we were getting from our new Agency tenants was very positive. We had some trouble at first as a result of Agencies not being good at moving into their new digs. They didn't have any recent experience and didn't anticipate the challenges, but once we introduced our "Move Management" process and staff to provide assistance, things smoothed out. Over four years we completed phase one and had garnered National recognition.

Five Thousand Workers, Work Better

I was convinced, office designs could have a positive effect on the work process, make the workplace a tool to enhance productivity, and had the potential to contribute to re-inventing the way people work.

The new State Satellite Office Complex grew to support almost 5,000 employees offering a modern work environment and the latest in technology infrastructure. I had always talked about the State being a long-term tenant and the building being designed for 100 years. After visiting the complex recently, it's been 25 years and they look as good as the day DMS moved in.

Two National
Innovation Awards

<33

NASFA

CSG The Council of State Governments

Be recognized by established organizations

It always helps to have people or organizations recognize the value of your innovation. You'll be the lead cheerleader for your idea but having outsiders praise your innovation can help credential your idea.

A lot had been accomplished. We had changed the culture of an Agency, moving from one that was seen as an inflexible Regulator to a Resource – focused on solving problems, always searching for a way to say yes. We had launched Florida government into the information age and made its internet portal number one in the Nation. And we had built the High Performance Workplace, making it a tool to increase occupant productivity. I had met my major goals and I could see the end of a fantastic ride was near.

We were in the last year of the Governor's second term. I wanted to go out with a bang but each day was getting less hectic and my schedule was becoming sparsely populated with fairly mediocre meetings. The quality of the day to day work was slipping as appointed managers had already left for other jobs or were working on their resumes.

Then, Lawton called. I assumed it was the traditional *thanks for your service* call. But, to my surprise, he gave me one more chance to do some "**Meaningful Work.**"

22 GOOD IDEAS SHOULD BE CROSS-POLLINATED

The SMART (Soundly Made, Accountable, Reasonable and Thrifty) school design initiative was funded by the Lottery to the tune of $600,000,000. But why? You would hope because elected officials were responding to an urgent need. Nice thought, but think again. The reason the SMART schools initiative happened was pressure from Florida Taxpayers.

Legislators were being pounded in their districts by their constituents, in Town Halls and on TV. The politicians who passed the Lottery into law assured the voters that funding to enhance education would be provided from revenue generated by the Lottery. So far, total dollars allocated – Zero.

The SMART initiative was passed into law by the legislature to fulfill their promise. Now it had to be implemented.<34

The legislation established a five-person commission to evaluate the school construction proposals and award the funds to those who qualified. Based on the legislation, the Governor could appoint the Chairman and one other member. He wanted to select someone he trusted and had knowledge of the construction business to Chair the Board. I turned out to be the lucky one.

My professional credentials as an Architect and head of the Agency responsible for the State's construction

TakeAway <34

Look for ways to cross-pollinate

One way to increase the impact of an innovation is to get others to adopt or leverage your methods.

Sharing resources builds market acceptance.

program were more than adequate. I knew construction. The Agency had created an evaluation process for it's *Incentives for Success* program that could be utilized by the Board. And the Building Construction team had been providing construction management services to city and county governments for several years. They had great cost data. By leveraging these assets, the newly established Smart Schools Commission was off to a quick start, reviewing and approving new school construction projects in less than 30 days.

The initiative was praised by the School Districts and, to the legislators' delight, the demonstrations to protest the lack of Lottery dollars for education had subsided.

SMART schools had produced positive results.

Collaboration between those having schools designed and built was a real benefit not only to control costs but also to learn what worked and what didn't.

SMART homepage searchable by Category, Location and Capacity

In addition, every recipient of funds was required to upload relative data (plans, costs, user comments, consultants, and other information) into a database accessible from the web.

The sharing of information helped lower costs and improve quality. But some argued the SMART school clearinghouse was just another bloated government program that had overreached its authority. <35 My contention was that government was playing a coordinative role to get the most out of taxpayers' dollars. The private sector, primarily contractors and architects, had another view – that the State was controlling the process and forcing the construction industry to be much less profitable.

The SMART school board was able to distribute $200,000,000 before the new political regime took power in Tallahassee. The initiative was shut down a week after inauguration. The remaining $400,000,000 was reallocated to "more worthwhile causes."

TakeAway <35

Don't assume your innovative work will be universally valued

You may be doing lots of good from your perspective but lots of damage from a different perspective. If you want your innovation to survive and thrive, be aware of different perspectives and search for common ground.

The impact on school construction was more than just the loss of funds although that was a real blow. The one-off custom school design solution, that always cost more, made a big comeback. But beyond costs escalating, the chance for collaboration, both face-to-face and on the web, to take advantage of the experience and accumulated knowledge of Florida's educators and facility experts was greatly diminished.

Serving in government, especially as the Secretary of DMS, I knew I had been given a gift – the opportunity to begin with a blank sheet and to be part of leading a revolution, of trying to Reinvent Government. The thrill ride for me would soon be over but I was sure what we had created, an online portal to serve our Citizens, a Workplace that improved productivity, and an Agency with a culture focused on SERVICE, these innovations would survive and continue to grow. I was sure that would be the case.

23 SUCCESSION-PLANNING MATTERS

TakeAway <36

Your innovation may need to become THEIR innovation

When your idea has broad appeal and customers have come to rely on what you offer, it can continue to function if an organization's new leadership makes minor changes and renames your creation making it their own. Don't see this as a negative. In this situation, your idea, now theirs, gets a second life.

The success of Government Services Direct, (GSD), our online application to bring services to the people, had made the DMS tech staff a target for private employers. The smart tech companies saw GSD as a model that could be commercialized.

But for Florida's next new leaders, the GSD infrastructure was not seen as THEIR <36 valuable asset to serve citizens and make government more efficient – but as just another attempt of government trying to do what should be left up to the professionals in the private sector.

Within a few months of the next administration taking power, similar to the SMART initiative, GSD was off-line and 90% of the talent had moved on, taking jobs in the private sector – most at triple their state salary.

GSD was sent to the digital scrap heap by a new administration, selling privatization as the key to an efficient (translation: minimal) government. Their stated agenda was captured in a quote from the new Governor's inauguration address: "We must empty these buildings of state workers." <37

83

Don't incite open hostility

Although the changes you believe are necessary will likely be disruptive to existing roles and rules, avoid public attacks.

A contract was executed with a private vendor, making the GSD domain, state.fl.us, a redirect to MyFlorida.com, the state's new portal.

The overall cost and effectiveness of the privatized system was hard to tie down, but most in the I.T. community felt it was considerably more expensive, not easily customized to meet the state's needs, and a lot less citizen friendly.

Many felt the spirit of innovation was no longer the *coin of the realm*. Perhaps this was just sour grapes, just another example of unwarranted resistance to change. But for the next 20 years, Florida was never considered a national tech leader.

Along with losing the position of technology innovator, Florida's High Performance Workplace initiative died. The innovative vision – The Workplace as a tool to improve productivity, was replaced by packing more people in less square footage and selling off state owned buildings when possible.

The most destructive blow to DMS was related to its culture. The department's employees had begun to believe being a public servant was something to be proud of. Helping other departments deliver services to Florida citizens was

"Those who govern, having much business on their hands, do not generally like to take the trouble of considering and carrying into execution new projects. The best public measures are therefore seldom adopted from previous wisdom, but forced by the occasion."
Ben Franklin

"meaningful work." That attitude was not shared by the new leadership in state government whose top priority was to put the private sector in charge of solving problems, not government. The newly elected officials asked a question I had also asked when I first arrived in Tallahassee – Why can't Government run like a Business? As a new arrival, I had felt the same but, over time, saw government quite differently. I was sorry to see history repeating itself.

24 DON'T ASSUME THEY'LL SEE IT LIKE YOU SEE IT

In addition to erasing what could be erased, *any* accomplishments that remained were seen as falling short. The new administration's assessments reminds me of a story I was told by a fellow public servant who worked with me in the Governor's office. When I was appointed the Secretary of DMS, he shared with me an experience he had in a similar job in Michigan government. His Governor had come to him with a question,

"Why do we have 22 print shops. That's crazy. Let's consolidate to 1 central print shop. We can save a ton of money."

The Governor had given him a directive. He leaped into action, meeting with Agencies, trying to find out why they needed their own printing operation. Everyone had a good reason. Everybody thought they were special. Really?

TakeAway <38

Don't expect your accomplishments to be recognized

Ben Franklin's accomplishments, even in the non-internet 18th century, were recognized world-wide. He died in his home in Philadelphia in 1790. You would assume his home would be treated as a national treasure. Wrong! Unfortunately, his grandchildren, who inherited his estate, had his home demolished and sold the property for commercial development.

85

He explained to me how he had gone through 3 legislative sessions writing bills each time to merge the print shops. But the Agencies had a different idea and had friends in the legislature. His first two attempts never even had a hearing in committee. He did all he could and finally got something enacted on the third try, reducing the print shops to 4. He told the Governor, who had decided not to run for a second term, and they both agreed it was time to declare victory.

His Governor left office and the new team came in to *make things right*. He was summoned by the new chief of staff. He thought, maybe this next group was interested in understanding what we had done that was working and what we had wanted to accomplish, but didn't. He was hopeful, but it was not a good sign that the meeting had been scheduled for just 5 minutes. The chief of staff had only one question,

"Why are there four print shops?" <38

EPILOGUE

It cannot be emphasized enough – putting Florida online, creating the High Performance Workplace and trying to Reinvent Government all happened at a moment in time when the planets were aligned.

But I have found, timing alone is not enough.
You must have the authority to act.

Governor Chiles had told me in his folksy, cracker style "as long as it ain't illegal or immoral, do what's in the best interest of the people." This type of untethered latitude is rare and I have since learned, it was essential for me to take risks, to drive change, to innovate, all while working in a bureaucratic organization.

25 ALWAYS BE READY FOR THE NEXT HOOP

While serving as the Secretary of the Department of Management Services, I was fortunate to meet and work with several influential leaders in positions of authority. Some would offer me opportunities to do "meaningful work" after my time in government had come to a close.

The most attractive offer was a position at a University. It was something I had not considered. I had been an Architect in the private sector, a manager in the public sector and now I was exploring an opportunuty in academia.

TakeAway <39

Expand your perspective before you take action

Always gather the facts before you finalize your innovation concept and begin implementation.

Review your research closely, identifying things you can adopt and things you'll need to avoid.

You'll see your innovation as original but rarely does anything start without assessing what has already been done.

Looking back, I remembered, Rhea had encouraged me to expand my portfolio from just being an Architect of buildings, to seeing Everything as a Design Problem. So I had a feeling this was the next Hoop.

I had met the President of the University, who had known Lawton for 30 years and became friends while serving in the Florida legislature. The President was part of a select group of Old Florida Crackers, Leaders who saw public service as a calling not a stepping stone to getting rich. I don't mean to imply that none of our elected officials are not trustworthy; it just seems statesmanship was more the norm in Lawton's generation. From the first moment I met the President, I knew he was offering me my next adventure, a chance to innovate, to be an Intrapreneur. We were going to explore a new mode of education – Distance Learning.

The President, Provost, Executive Director of the Community College system and I went on a field trip to the British Open University (Lawton would have called it a Fact-Finding mission). The British Open University was seen as the world leader in home study, now Distance Learning. We were there for 3 days, each day packed with a full agenda. We were exhausted as we boarded our flight back to Atlanta but were also exhilarated.<39

We all saw this as a delivery method that had enormous potential and the President had a role for me. He asked if I would join him in formulating an approach for FSU and then help implement the University's Distance Learning Program.

I said to myself "Of course I wanted to be on his team." I didn't say it out loud, but I wanted to make sure it was the right fit, that my talents matched the task before I made a final commitment. I shared with him what I saw as the ultimate goal – to ensure Floridians were Always Learning – and specifically for the University, that our students could Learn Anytime and Anyplace, and ultimately, that the Content would match the individual learner's profile.

This was an audacious goal, the kind of goal I embraced with enthusiasm. The President and I shared the vision that Distance Learning was going to have a real impact on education and invited me again to help him shape the University's approach.

The Chiles' administration was winding down. In 45 days a new Governor would take over and bring in his people, a team that would not likely include me. I told the President I was in. But I had Leaped with Lawton having only a potential of finding meaningful work. At this point, I was hoping for a little more clarity. I asked if we could meet to set the general framework of my new role at the University. He said that sounded good.

TakeAway <40

Look to balance Risk with Stability

Don't be risk averse, but the key advantages of being an Intrapreneur is access to resources – capital and personnel, and a permanent position with salary and benefits.

I had learned in the Governor's office that to be an effective innovator, you needed an institutionally respected title and staff. Distance Learning was exciting and would be the future, but its funding was not determined and the staffing would be initially sparse. Don't get me wrong, I love StartUps – they are exciting – but I wanted both: the risk-taking of StartUps with the stability of an Institution. In reflection, I now could see I was cut out to be an Intrapreneur – working like a StartUp within a large organization. <40

I searched the University's website and found a few units that might work as the Institutional component of my job. One really fit for a non-academic, an Architect/State worker – the Center for Professional Development (CPD). Its customers were adult learners, a big market for Distance Learning, and because it wasn't an academic unit, the faculty wouldn't push back on a non-PhD director. It was housed in a freestanding building – the Florida State Conference Center, located on the edge of campus. It was part of the campus but also close to the Capitol, a place where I had contacts I could leverage. It had a mission I could get my head around – to extend the resources of the University, and it had troops – 60 staff on the payroll.

I met with the President, expressed my need for a full plate, and suggested I could do three things: run the CPD programs, manage the Conference Center, and help to energize the Distance Learning Program. And one more thing that I hoped would not be a deal breaker: I had been asked to do some consulting work for a Telco in Atlanta and had got the impression from my discussions with the President that this type of outside activity would be permissible.

As I asked to have a full plate, I couldn't help thinking of a poster hanging on the wall of my storage room office in the Mansion years ago, when I had first arrived in Tallahassee. It was a gift from Rhea: a drawing of a bug leaning up against a huge piece of cake, 10 times its size. The bug had been gorging and had managed to consume twice its weight, but only putting a small dent in the cake. The bug's stomach was bulging and it looked exhausted leaning against the cake. I've never forgot the saying:

Always take on more than you can possibly do, or you'll never do all you can.

The President was happy with the ambitious job description I proposed but wanted a few details related to the consulting work. I outlined what the Telco company was after. They wanted to leverage my experiences while serving in State government. The President was agreeable. In fact, he thought this type of outside activity would more complement than conflict with my university duties. We shook hands, the old school version of signing a legally binding contract, and he set my start date to coincide with me leaving DMS. I was filled with anticipation, ready to jump to the next Hoop.

I arrived on campus with the same spirit I had when I started in government. I was working for a leader in the Lawton Chiles' tradition. I felt sure the work would be meaningful, and I was still passionate about making a difference.

"Being the richest man in the cemetery doesn't matter to me. Going to bed at night saying we've done something wonderful, that's what matters to me."
Steve Jobs

90

26 WORK WITH WHAT YOU KNOW <41

TakeAway <41

Built on what you know works

If you have experience with a technology tool or a proven method of getting something done, you should use it because you know it works.

But a note of caution: Keep your eyes open for the next new thing that will make your proven approach obsolete.

I wanted to follow the same path I had at DMS - start with listening, not talking. I had planned for a 30-day get-a-feel-for-things period, but the easy does it approach was going to end abruptly.

After 2 weeks on the job, the Provost, who I reported to, summoned me to his office and began sharing how the President had bragged on my problem-solving skills, how I had practically reinvented government, making it work better and cost less, and that I was a great addition to the university. I was starting to get suspicious. Where was he going with this? At the university everybody is smart, especially him. Then he dropped the bomb.

27 HOUSEKEEPING COMES FIRST

The Provost said he had been looking at CPD for quite a while, a fact not disclosed when I was recruited. He believed CPD needed some major changes and he laid out the assignment: He wanted to reduce the staff by 50% and, at the same time, expand the adult-learner market. He set the timetable to align with the budget cycle, which gave me 10 months. Oh yea, and he was also looking for me to help launch the Distance Learning program, ramping up the online course offerings. He had been on the trip to the British Open University, was on-board big time, and wanted to get the university in the game.

OK, I could see this was going to eat up a lot of my band width and could certainly cause me to have a rocky start at CPD. My outward demeanor was calm and I said, give me a few days to gather some data and pull a plan together. He said fine, how's the end of next week? That gave me 8 days. Seemed doable, after all, I had engineered the creation of the hurricane Andrew $4 billion presentation in 7 days. Compared, this would be a snap. As I took the 10 minute walk back to my office I got less cocky. But this was something I was good at – thinking on the fly, being able to improvise.

28 WHAT IT TAKES TO STREAMLINE AN ORGANIZATION

To streamline and reorganize an organization I always ask two questions:

> Is the work we do the work we need ?
>
> How do we make the work less work ?

This two-pronged approach to rethinking the work had become central whenever I face the need for radical change.

The first step is to make sure *the work we do is the work we need*. You can make something more efficient but that something may be the wrong thing. My way to look at this is you can make the trains go from station to station faster, but are they going to the right stations? After you have aligned the work with the organization's mission, and made sure the funding is in place to support the mission as defined, then you go to step two – *make the work less work*.

Today, making the work less work is driven by applying technology. What took a week to accomplish pre-networked-computers and pre-internet can now happen in a few minutes.

I put in a few long days (and nights) but I felt I had put together a workable approach.

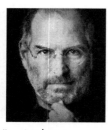

As promised, I showed up in six days with a plan. I covered how we would refocus our mission, eliminating stuff that we didn't need to do, allowing us to reduce the staff over a 6-to-9-month period.

I also outlined how we would employ technology to dramatically streamline the process of doing the needed work.

"...And it comes from saying no to 1,000 things to make sure we don't get on the wrong track or try to do too much. We're always thinking about new markets we could enter, but it's only by saying no that you can concentrate on the things that are really important".
Steve Jobs

I asked for an allocation to fund the technology needed to streamline the process. The provost listened closely and reviewed the plan I presented. He agreed with the overall plan and to fund the technology but wanted a progress report every 60 days. I agreed. From my perspective, regular updates were good, they would help me to keep the pressure on and if I ran into something unexpected, I could propose a mid-course correction. I left to get started with sorting out the work needed.

Is the work we do the work we need

To reduce the CPD staff by 50% in 10 months could not be done by attrition alone. I would need to eliminate work that did not directly support the mission. I created a road map, sorting the current functions into what I needed to keep and what I had to offload.

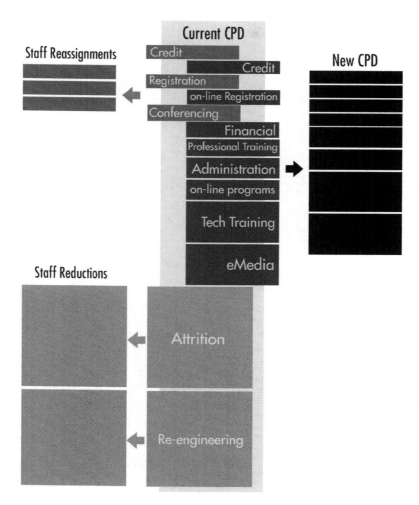

It took a little longer than I had planned to streamline the staff, 14 months instead of 10, but I think the Provost thought it might take 2 years but gave me a tight deadline to create a sense of urgency. While I was rethinking the work and reducing the payroll, I formulated the way to apply technology to make the work less work.

OLD PROCESS

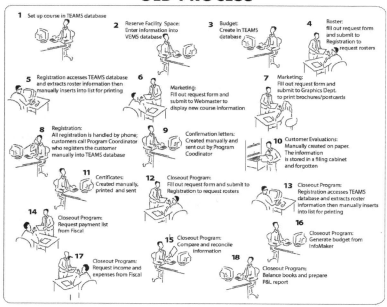

1 Set up course in TEAMS database

2 Reserve Facility Space:
Enter information into
VEMS database

3 Budget:
Create in TEAMS
database

4 Roster:
fill out request form
and submit to
Registration to
request rosters

5 Registration accesses TEAMS database
and extracts roster information then
manually inserts into list for printing

6 Marketing:
Fill out request form and
submit to Webmaster to
display new course information

7 Marketing:
Fill out request form and
submit to Graphics Dept.
to print brochures/postcards

8 Registration:
All registration is handled by phone;
customers call Program Coordinator
who registers the customer
manually into TEAMS database

9 Confirmation letters:
Created manually and
sent out by Program
Coodinator

10 Customer Evaluations:
Manually created on paper.
The information
is stored in a filing cabinet
and forgotten

11 Certificates:
Created manually,
printed and sent

12 Closeout Program:
Fill out request form and submit to
Registration to request rosters

13 Closeout Program:
Registration accesses TEAMS
database and extracts roster
information then manually inserts
into list for printing

14 Closeout Program:
Request payment list
from Fiscal

15 Closeout Program:
Compare and reconcile
information

16 Closeout Program:
Generate budget from
InfoMaker

17 Closeout Program:
Request income and
expenses from Fiscal

18 Closeout Program:
Balance books and prepare
P&L report

NEW PROCESS

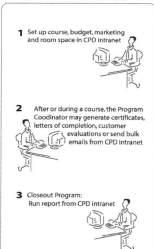

1 Set up course, budget, marketing
and room space in CPD intranet

2 After or during a course, the Program
Coodinator may generate certificates,
letters of completion, customer
evaluations or send bulk
emails from CPD intranet

3 Closeout Program:
Run report from CPD intranet

How do we make the work less work

I put the CPD leadership team through a series of brainstorming sessions. At the end of our 4th session we came up with an initiative we called **PALMS** (the Professional Adult Learning Management System).

It would become a customizable Dash-Board.

My time in State government had made me a true believer that if you give people the best computer and the best software and pay attention to lighting and ergonomics, people will be more productive. Now I wanted to take the next Leap. To Create a software that allows each employee to customize their desktop <42, to present the tools that they need to do their work. It would be a modular system that allowed each user to "drop and drag" the modules that help them do the job. For example, the facilities manager would need the room layout module to plan and set the room layouts for clients. The Finance officer would need the budget control module, the registration module and the refunds module. PALMS provided a Dash-Board interface, configured by the user to match the workflow and tasks derived from their unique scope of work. By eliminating work that was not part of our defined mission, getting rid of scope creep and customizing the user interface, and creating PALMS to match the necessary tasks to the person responsible, we were reinventing CPD.

TakeAway <42

The new target market is ONE

Whatever your target market, personalization is key. It's not enough to sell three sizes, small, medium, and large. You need to customize for the individual. People want a process that automatically adjusts to fit their unique perspective. Whenever possible, create a solution that can address each user or buyer's specific needs.

Something I realized at the end of the PALMS 10-year life cycle – it had institutionalized the work process. The PALMS application was the CPD playbook we all relied on to work efficiently. It was a stabilizing force.

At decommissioning, it still worked well. It was difficult for the CPD team to give it up. They relied on PALMS to do their work and, as do most who face change, they resisted. But the code had been written in a language that was obsolete and the University's software infrastructure had been updated, causing the link between the two systems to be broken beyond repair. I had second thoughts and began to design

PALMS 2.0. But after a few weeks, we shut it down and faced the fact that it was time to turn the page. **<43** Ten years was a good run, and I now appreciate the death of any innovation as part of the process. When old systems die, it opens the door for the next Leap, a chance for us or the next innovator to innovate.

TakeAway <43

Don't let your Innovation be dislodged too soon but be ready to let go

You want to ensure your innovation has a reasonable shelf life. But be aware of changing conditions and user expectations. If your innovation is beyond being re-tooled, be willing to move on – letting your initial idea be retired.

I felt I had come a long way in revitalizing CPD and was getting good feedback from around campus. The unit had laid dormant for years but now it had clearly defined why it was an important part of the University's mission. The University proper was taking care of the students during their 4-year campus experience, CPD was focused on extending the resources of the University to insure our graduates were Always Learning. I'm convinced CPD's charge is especially critical in today's rapidly changing environment. CPD was on track, but what happen to the Telco consulting deal?

The initial assignment from the Provost to restructure CPD was near completion. I was committed to continuous improvement at CPD – implementing technology based solutions to make the organization more efficient and serve more adult learners but, I felt there was now time in my schedule to begin the consulting work I had been approved to do when I first came on board.

I made a call to see if the offer was still on the table and if I could make it work without disrupting my responsibilities at the university.

The Private Sector can learn from the Public Sector

The telecommunications company I had been asked to consult with was headquartered in Atlanta. The senior VP of operations, who had the lion's share of employees in his chain of command (50,000) and reported directly to the company's President, had made me a good offer. I could be in Atlanta every other Friday and do work from home as needed. That gave me the flexibility to work in bursts as needed, cutting down on travel and my out of office time. I Leaped into this new adventure as always, hoping to innovate.

As had been the case when I arrived in government, I was not greeted with open arms from the Telco's Department heads. "What the hell does this outsider, this old government bureaucrat, know about our business?" **<44** As it was, I couldn't claim to be an expert, but I knew more than they expected. My Agency, DMS, managed the delivery of the State's voice and data service when I served in State government. The Division of Communications was responsible for their company's annual eight-figure Telecommunications contract. I spent time reviewing these contracts and meeting with upper management.

TakeAway <44

Innovation from outside

Not being an insider does make some aspects of bringing about change more difficult. But being an outsider is not always bad. If you've been given a defined role that might include the authority to evaluate, make recommendations, and lead the prescribed change, being an outsider can be empowering. Outsiders are seen with skepticism, but if you persist and maintain the confidence of a well plugged-in sponsor, you can have an impact.

I had gotten to know the Telco's V.P. pretty well through participating in the contract review sessions. Turned out, he was a college roommate of the Governor's Chief of Staff. They had gone to the University of Florida as had I. He had been to our offices in the Capitol on several occasions and had observed firsthand the innovative initiatives I was leading – putting Florida on-line, developing the High Performance Workplace, changing government culture – moving from a Regulator to a Resource. He recognized the value I was adding to a large institution and wanted to infuse my Intrapreneurial experience into his similar-sized enterprise.

TakeAway <45

Focus - don't shoot in all directions, pick your target

You'll want to have a broad perspective of the enterprise system's overall mission and structure. But don't try to take everything on at once. Find a rich target where resistance is low, the cost to act is reasonable, and you can show incremental success quickly. Once you have a win in your column, look to diversity and ramp up the attack.

Like government, his operation had lots of rules and people who were happy with the way they had always done things. The challenges he faced fit my portfolio.

Lots of processes needed streamlining at the Telco, but as I listened to the V.P., I could see one critical need. **<45** He had to have a pipeline of talented new recruits to join the company if they were to sustain their leadership in the industry. I proposed to focus on the OnBoarding process, including finding, training and infusing the critical new blood into the enterprise. The V.P. said go for it.

It took longer than I had hoped, but the process of OnBoarding was transformed into a web-powered application that reinvented finding, training, and retaining talent. I was able to meddle in several other areas – working on their

99

High Performance regional office parks and their Incentives for Success program. I had accomplished a lot – helping to reinvent a highly regulated and bureaucratic private sector business, but it was time to call it a day.

The Center for Professional Development was running smoothly, rolling out more online offerings, ramping up the conferencing services and applying innovative web capture and conversion technologies to deliver web assisted learning. But with the consulting work over, I saw another opportunity to innovate on the horizon. The universities Tech Transfer Unit was exploring how to tap into a new vehicle to export university Innovations – the Tech Incubator. I got the go-ahead to explore developing an e-business incubator.

30 THE DIGITAL GOLD RUSH

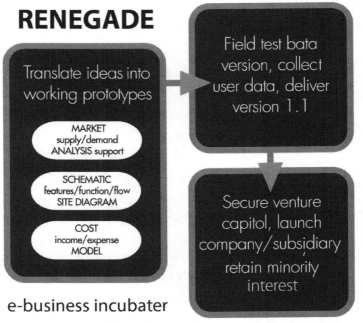

RENEGADE

Translate ideas into working prototypes

MARKET
supply/demand
ANALYSIS support

SCHEMATIC
features/function/flow
SITE DIAGRAM

COST
income/expense
MODEL

Field test bata version, collect user data, deliver version 1.1

Secure venture capitol, launch company/subsidiary retain minority interest

e-business incubater

Renegade was established to translate innovative dot com ideas into successful businesses.

The dot-com boom ran roughly from 1995 to 2001. The formula was simple: get the largest share of a market segment as fast as possible without worrying about cash flow, without a ROI strategy except the promise of monetizing somewhere down the road. In retrospect, it sounded crazy.

Turned out, it was.

I pulled together some investors and bought a 4,000 sq. ft. building adja- cent to campus. We were going to launch an incubator positioned to attract talent from the University. I coordinated with our Tech Transfer Unit who was anxious to help us connect to internet entrepreneurs. The facility was subdivided into six studios offered for rent to internet startups. We kept one for our own startup, Renegade Digital Development, and quickly rented the other five spaces. Our business model was built, as was most dot-coms, on the misguided logic that with market share would come making a profit. It was an exciting time with most studios operat- ing on a 24-hour basis.

By 2001, just 24 months of managing to ride the wave, the boom went bust. Some major dot-com players' stock value dropped overnight from $700 per share to $7 per share. A few survived, but Renegade went down like the Titanic.<46

Our few paying clients pulled the plug and no new prospects appeared on the horizon. In 90 days, the company's incubator building was vacant. It was a great location so we were able to sell it for use as a traditional office building with tenants that *didn't include start-ups*. It had been a roller-coaster ride, a thrill, but it was over. Venture Capitalists were now only funding new companies that had a solid Return On Investment (ROI).

> **"When in doubt, don't."**
> *Ben Franklin*

31 ADAPT OR PERISH

It would take several years for launching new internet businesses to be back in vogue, but online education was hot. CPD had been in early, but the market was quickly getting crowded and, to stay competitive, we needed to step up our game. I was looking for an edge. We had a respected brand – a major University's seal that could be affixed to a professional certification. That imprimatur had real value. But the online courses available in the market had exploded over the last 5 years, many of high quality and offered by reputable providers. We were on par in terms of quality, but how could we drive our cost down to beat the competition? My gut told me we had to speed up the course development process, cutting costs in order to be competitive.

First, I began to compile data. CPD's on-line courses were taking 3 to 4 months to develop at a cost of around $200,000 upfront dollars for each course. Four years ago, we had professional development offerings for State Agencies where they paid the upfront

TakeAway <47

Stay aware of changing conditions

New circumstances can provide new opportunities or, if not addressed, can derail or even kill an existing initiative. Always be assessing the Future State.

development costs and shared the revenue stream as the courses were sold. One generated a very nice revenue stream – $50,000 per year. Today, that type of deal wouldn't fly. The online component of our portfolio had dried up. We were caught asleep at the wheel and needed to find a replacement for this lost revenue.

I started to reassess our circumstances. What had changed? <47 Oh yea, the internet was no longer a novelty – it was the core of the information sharing society. We were in the internet age, unlimited relevant content was seen as free and instantly available by keyword search. The old pay upfront, take-months-to-deliver business model was obsolete. We had to find a new approach to course development that was built on the internet business framework – I tried to boil down the essence of a new approach;

- launch your innovation with no up-front money
- move from concept to delivery FAST
- produce a revenue stream to fund ongoing costs

I called the new course development method **Rapid Skills Development.** <48

A lot of implementation details were worked out over the next year, capturing the content and converting the raw materials to credentialed training. RSD had a strong internet business bone structure and we were confident we were on the right path. It was uncertain RSD was the next big thing, but we were convinced the old model was dead. It was now all about marketing.

TakeAway <48

The internet business model can be the key

You must consider three principles if your innovation is to be internet-business-compliant. Be able to launch your innovation with little or no up-front money; be able to move from concept to delivery FAST; and ensure that new business must be able to produce a continuous revenue stream to fund its ongoing costs.

RSD is used to capture and convert presentations to online courses quickly and eco-nomically.

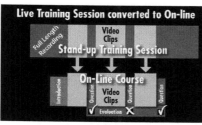

RSD uses the Inter-net Business Model to generate a reve-nue stream that helps sustain CPD's professional devel-opment programs.

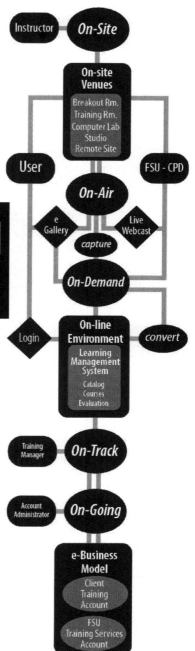

32 SPINNING MORE THAN ONE PLATE

Without question, being part of the university had offered me a broad array of innovative experiences. Although I now lived by the mantra – *Everything is a Design Problem*, I was still, at my core, an Architect. And Architects have a predisposition for the design and construction of buildings. As it turned out, I would get a chance to apply my professional training to another development project.

My partner in the Governor's Inn hotel called and wanted me to join him in a potential project. He had found a parcel that could be developed and wanted me to do the conceptual design and a feasibility analysis. Opportunity was knocking, and I agreed to take a look provided this was an allowable outside activity. I saw a fit.

In the back of my mind, I had always wanted to teach an advanced course about Real Estate Development and this development project could provide the content for an interesting course.

I got to work putting together some initial numbers. Based on my calculations, it seemed there was real potential. My former hotel partner, who would lead the new project's development effort, identified some potential investors who could provide the capital. He was not one to hesitate. He got an option on the property. We ran a few trap-lines focused on market demand. Was this the time to re-enter the development business? I agreed to participate as long as I could limit my time to more of a consulting role.

The project envisioned delivering a waterfront resort that had multiple components: 50 condos, a restaurant on the river, a ship's store, dockage, a pavilion over the water for special events, and a community pool. We set our sights at creating *a fisherman's paradise*.

Again, as with the earlier hotel project, I assumed the role of designer and numbers-cruncher, charged with delivering an outstanding design solution that customers loved *and* a project that would make a reasonable profit. For me, it was important to strike a balance between striving to meet or even exceed the customers' expectations and maximizing profit for yourself and your investors. My partner nailed down the investors and signed the contract to purchase the property.

View from the property looking out the Carrabelle River to the Gulf of Mexico.

After 60 days conducting our due diligence, the new project's LLC owned a spectacular waterfront property.

This project would offer a chance to revive the "Old Florida" tradition. The *LOOK* started with a sketch.

We had a checklist, covering every detail, specifying who does what and when. We were the project's managers and had control. We were the masters of the universe. And when we had executed contracts for 40 of the 50 units the first weekend, we were convinced we had hit a home run. We let up on the gas and planned to coast to the finish-line.<49

TakeAway <49

Instant success can lead to disaster

Obviously, you want to grow your initiative as fast as possible. Meeting demand promptly is critical, but you must balance supply and demand and may get the best results by managing growth.

Income & Expense Estimate

EXPENSES	
Marketing & Sales	$943,500
Development Fee	$464,000
Property acquisition	$3,500,000
Property Carry Cost (interest only)	$333,000
Architecture & Engineering	$195,175
Surveying	$18,500
Legal	$150,000
Site Improvements	$500,000
Contract Labor	$50,000
Demolition	$150,000
Water & Sewer Fees	$250,000
Permit and Processing Fees	$95,000
Project Management Fee (36 mos.)	$296,000
Bookkeeping & Accounting	$130,500
Contingency	$440,000
Unit Construction	$5,568,000
Restaurant renovation	$450,000
Dry Slips	$535,500
TOTAL EXPENSES	$14,069,175
INCOME	
Lot & Slip Sales	$5,930,000
Unit Sales	$10,800,000
Restaurant Sale	$1,500,000
TOTAL INCOME	$18,230,000
Total Net Cash (includes investor cash)	$5,160,777

It's much more likely the project design will not be *Value Engineered* to cut costs if the Architect can convince his client that the solution is driven by his cash flow.

Development Schedule

Pirates Landing																													
YEAR	2004											2005												2006					
MONTHLY	1	2	3	4	5	6	7	8	9	10	11	12	13	14	15	16	17	18	19	20	21	22	23	24	25	26	27	28	29
			sales																										
						construction														Punch List Close Out									
							unit closings																	Turnover Condo					

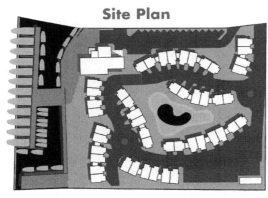

Site Plan

When Architects can run the numbers and project the clients' Profit expectations, the Architect will be better equipped to control design scope creep, which will help to insure the project will get built.

Aerial of Project

Comparison of proposed site plan to actual construction.

You Can't Predict the Unpredictable

Six months later we were 75% complete and on track. Our assumptions were within 2%, the cash flow was positive, all was going as planned. We were counting the money.

Then the unexpected hit. It was the worst hurricane season in my lifetime. It did major damage to the site infrastructure and some of the units. Materials stored on the site were destroyed or washed away.

2005 Hurricane Season

Dennis - July 10
Emily - July 17
Katrina - 28 August
Rita - 23 September
Wilma - 21 October

The natural disaster caused almost all the buyers to break their contract (so much for legal obligations) and walk. The buyers loved the project when they bought in, but they had lost their appetite for coastal living and wanted out. The construction had stopped, most of the buyers were gone, and the interest clock was running at $40,000 a month.

It looked unlikely we could turn things around. Luckily, the current value of the property was more than the remaining debt – so we negotiated with the bank and settled. On the bright side, the project's Architecture was something to brag about, but the financial outcome – not so much. It was a two-year effort with no financial reward. It wasn't easy to let it go, but we had to chalk it up as a learning experience.

My time as Developer was over. The outcome was less than we had hoped, but the experience had taught me some valuable lessons. Lessons that I thought were worth sharing.

33 SHARING MY LEARNING EXPERIENCE

There was one silver lining to my 2nd act as a Developer – as I had speculated, the experience would make a great course. It would allow me to refocus on what I saw as CPD's central mission – extend the resources of the university so Floridians are **Always Learning**. Teaching would give me an opportunity to share a real-world experience with those looking for a career in Real Estate Development. I put together the curriculum and worked with the university's Housing Science program to offer a master's level course titled Residential Development. It was offered both to students who needed credit and to professionals who wanted CEU's. It was a 3-credit-hour course offered fall semester. Fifteen registered – 10 FSU students and 5 professionals: 2 Architects, 2 real estate brokers, and a home builder. I was pleased with the response and the mix of both students with professionals.

In reflecting on my role as a teacher, I realized an important part of the learning experience comes from the dialog between the professionals and the students. This made the studio sessions interactive conversations, *not* lectures. I realized the face to face component was critical. I became a strong proponent of the Hybrid-Formatted* course.

> * Hybrid-Formatted courses take advantage of the best features of both traditional face-to-face "seat time" *and* online learning activities. They are also referred to as Blended Courses.

In addition to dialog, the course featured a hands-on team project. Each 3-person team, 2 students and 1 professional, selected a property and proposed a development plan. They were evaluated based on their participation in the class discussion *and* the Development Package they submitted. (It reminded me of the initiative I had launched while I was in government – CPR – Cross-functional, Project-driven, Results-oriented.) Teaching was gratifying, but with only 15 students per class, it didn't have the big impact I was searching for.

I wanted to explore an institution-wide initiative, one that would have an impact on the entire campus – all of its 40,000 students.

The next innovative challenge would be driven by another byproduct of the internet age – allowing anyone to access anything, any time.

Instant gratification was now in the art of the possible. I drew on what we had done with PALMS – information was tailored to each employee's specific job tasks. What if we applied that level of personalization to our Campus-bound student population? What if we created a living and learning environment where

Students could get exactly what they needed, exactly when they needed it? With this as the central organizing principle, the Digital Campus Initiative was born.

111

THE
DIGITAL CAMPUS

I jumped in with the usual wild enthusiasm that is part of exploring a new idea, but I forgot one of the past key ingredients: the endorsement and public support of the organization's top leadership, in this case the President of the university. But I did have a relationship with someone who would play a central role in developing the infrastructure for the initiative.

I had become a close friend with the university's Chief Information Officer (CIO). About once a month we would have lunch and share ideas about how to enhance campus IT services. I rolled out my Digital Campus idea with him and for the next several months it was a topic added to our lunch BS sessions. After each discussion, and with more research on what was in the art of the possible, I began to refine the idea.

34 ENVISIONING A STUDENT-CENTRIC CAMPUS

I wanted to think big and I knew the transformation I was after would not happen overnight. I thought it would take over a decade. It would be an enterprise-level initiative likely resisted by a lot of stakeholders already invested in their own ideas of the future. If I had any chance of success, I would need to be relentless, build departmental support, grow stakeholders, and be patient. It would be a test, can an Intrapreneur with little institutional authority make a large bureaucracy embrace such a long-term initiative?

"Energy and persistence conquer all things."
Ben Franklin

My poster child to help put a face on my vision of the future came from a photo of Sydney, the niece of a co-worker. She's 3 years old and she already knows how to swipe. In 2030, when she is a freshman in college, she'll have high expectations that must be met if the Campus experience is to survive. Will we be ready to give her exactly what she needs, exactly when she needs it?

Sydney already knows how to swipe on an iPhone

My initial idea was mostly about the digital connection but, being an Architect, one who enjoyed walking the Campus almost every day, I was convinced we had to do more. I envisioned a Campus experience that fully integrated the Physical and Virtual environment.

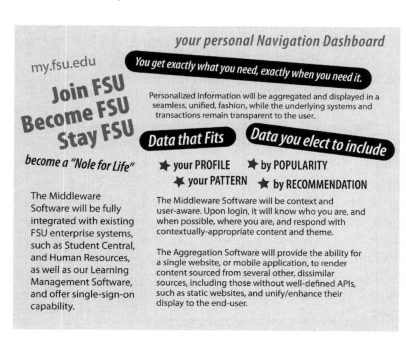

your personal Navigation Dashboard

my.fsu.edu

Join FSU
Become FSU
Stay FSU

become a "Nole for Life"

You get exactly what you need, exactly when you need it.

Personalized information will be aggregated and displayed in a seamless, unified, fashion, while the underlying systems and transactions remain transparent to the user.

Data that Fits   **Data you elect to include**

★ your PROFILE   ★ by POPULARITY
★ your PATTERN   ★ by RECOMMENDATION

The Middleware Software will be fully integrated with existing FSU enterprise systems, such as Student Central, and Human Resources, as well as our Learning Management Software, and offer single-sign-on capability.

The Middleware Software will be context and user-aware. Upon login, it will know who you are, and when possible, where you are, and respond with contextually-appropriate content and theme.

The Aggregation Software will provide the ability for a single website, or mobile application, to render content sourced from several other, dissimilar sources, including those without well-defined APIs, such as static websites, and unify/enhance their display to the end-user.

When I shared my concerns about the future survival of the place, the brick-and-mortar campus, most shrugged their shoulders and said, "This Campus has been here for over a hundred years, and it will be here for hundreds more. Don't be such an alarmist." I remember when Kodak celebrated its hundred-year anniversary. What happened when the world went digital? They were effectively gone. But I was not alone with my concerns. There was some evidence that it could happen – learning anywhere without a dedicated place, learning anytime not on a preset class schedule, but on demand.

Some were predicting that going to campus would be re-placed by going online. I was not a big believer in on-site and online being comparable experiences. I saw the value in putting learning resources online to support some aspects of learning, but not as a replacement for the real-world, Campus experience.

Perhaps I'm a little over the line with my fear that the physical Campus could be gone in a few decades, but there are reports that some small colleges are already closing their doors. They are no longer a viable business, especially as public funding is drying up.

If Distance Learning, along with the cost of higher education, continue to grow, I see many more campus closings. But I plan to combat that trend. I'm convinced that physical place will continue to be a powerful part of the learning experience – especially if we can link place to the digital environment.

I want our University to embrace the new digital delivery of content. But I also see leveraging the network to include the "internet of things" and to connect space with time. OK, I know the space/time thing is a little much, but bear with me. Here's what I'm thinking; a digital umbrella, a wireless canopy will enclose the campus. Where students are and when they are there will trigger pushing the right information to the specific students. Whether it's a special lecture getting started just 50 yards from where they're walking or a 50%-off deal for a slice of pizza at the food truck parked at the next corner, they get a custom communication. The push message – text, images, audio, or even video – fits them personally; it's matched to their unique profiles. <50

I had in mind a Digital Campus that embraced technology to support the living and learning experience, but was fully integrated with the physical environment. When Sydney arrives on our campus we'll know her. She'll have the freedom to explore but always have a digital compass in her pocket. She can choose to opt-out, but the benefits to participate will be substantial.

Initially I needed to share my idea beyond my lunch BS sessions with the CIO. I put together a tri-fold to build awareness. That was fine; it helped to make it real, but I wanted to create a sense of urgency. I knew that was a tall order with such a big, enterprise-wide idea that was focused way in the future – 2030. I tried to outline the story starting with the present state and walking us into the future.

Will we be ready for the Class of 2030?

For Our University to ensure its Residential Campus Experience remains viable, it must meet the expectations of the ever growing population of digitally savvy students. They see the world as "on-demand," ready when they are. They ask "What's the holdup?"

For the University to attract our future campus occupants, it must invest in fully integrating the physical and virtual environment. This means the Living and Learning Environment embodied in the Campus Experience must be "aware" – ready to react in real-time with personalized information that meets the needs of every individual student in residence. The path forward is unclear for On-Campus education but the Technology leadership at FSU is beginning to lay the foundation for the "Wired Campus." The question is, will we be ready?

2015 *Today's freshman class was born just as "the internet took everyone onto the information highway." While these students were in elementary, middle school, and high school, universities were establishing distance learning programs offering online courses, full online degrees, and e-services to support campus life. This class arrived on campus with basic expectations that all living and learning campus services would be accessible online and through any device. But this connectivity wasn't quite there yet.*

Campus administrators were contemplating the future of higher education. What will be the impact of MOOCS (Massive Open Online Courses)? How will the "new" knowledge work and the ever-strengthening job market forces impact the learning model? And how will educational institu-

tions reinvent their traditional models of education to leverage this new era of technology? And, as it turns out, we are not alone. New players were appearing. The private sector was mounting a challenge. Corporations were not only asking similar strategic questions, but also making large investments in the next big ideas and partnerships. Disney invested over $1 billion in Big Data tied to wearable technology to maximize their visitors' park experience with what I believe had parallels to a campus experience. Business-oriented social networks like LinkedIn, with a 1.5 billion dollar purchase of Lynda.com, were adding e-learning divisions to corner the market on connecting skills development to jobs.

2020 By the time the freshman of 2015 graduate and the class of 2020 enrolls, online degree graduates will have gained equal status with campus-bound graduates in the job market. Employers are offering career-to-courses "alignment" data to help ensure job placement. Universities are offering student portfolios to match course objectives to employer requirements. Some higher education institutions are considering "unbundling" degrees to provide an instructional track to better match specific job market requirements. Educational values that lead to career success such as "always learning" and "critical thinking" are being emphasized. Universities are beginning to address the growing gap between graduate skills and existing business needs. They also are doubling their efforts to offer continuous learning opportunities for their graduates over the life of their career, working to keep the University connected to their graduates.

And there is a growing challenge: Non-traditional entities are offering educational "credentialing," using competency evaluations that match the requirements of business and providing employers a new source of "ready-to-work" employees. While some campuses are closing their doors, for thriving campuses it is becoming clear that the emerging student profile of Generation Z expects a customized, immersive physical and virtual environment. Campus administrators must rethink the "campus experience" in order to meet the changing student expectations of these digital natives. Their needs go way beyond basic web access and simple online financial transactions. The University has begun to respond, deploying a digital strategy for students to "join, become, and stay" at FSU. The IT team continues to roll out an even more mobile-friendly interface with a larger set of apps to support campus life.

2025   This group of freshman grew up on their parent's Facebook wall from day one. Over the last 10 years, FSU has been getting prepared for the "all the time, every place" connected freshman class. Florida State invested in the infrastructure in 2015 to deliver what they called "The Digital Campus." They were convinced in 2015 that the students of the future would expect to get "just the information they needed exactly when they needed it." Their individual Profile, Living and Learning Pattern, Geo-location, and Selected Special Interests would always be there to help guide their actions. The campus was now blanketed with "beacons" to tie location to targeted push messaging. Leveraging digital assets as well as new education paradigms such as "unbundling" of degrees provides the customization that this class and their future employers are demanding. They see "The Digital Campus" not as a luxury, but a basic requirement.

2030   As predicted over a decade ago, more than 25% of campuses closed or drastically reduced their offerings. But FSU was thriving. Its leadership had made critical infrastructure investments back in 2015. FSU's vision for a "Digital Campus," where students expected a customized experience and immersive environment to Live and Learn, was a game-

changer. FSU was the number one Wired Campus in America and seen as a truly "Student-Centric" environment.

I felt the *"sense of urgency pitch"* worked, but the future of The Digital Campus initiative was still uncertain.

Creating a Framework for Implementation

In 2015, The Digital Campus got its first funding – $500,000. The IT team was pretty fired up. Getting a financial commitment made it real. Funding sent the signal that the initiative was important to leadership. But, even though the money was put in the IT department's budget, I cautioned them that this was <u>not</u> a technology initiative. Technology would be critical to support the user experience, but the Digital Campus would utilize the constant connection to information to make the student's real-world, living-and-learning experience better, much better.

The departments, who all shared the mission of making students successful, would need to be convinced that this initiative would complement, even strengthen, what they were doing and that, collectively, all Departments would benefit. To be realistic, this would be a tough sell.

By the middle of 2016, resistance was growing. As with all change, especially at the enterprise level, the organizational units, working independently, felt they were doing what needed to be done and doing it well. And besides, 2030 is a long way out; what about next semester or next year? As I predicted, it's hard to think long-term when the day-to-day challenges are sapping your energy.

The CIO's team had lots of talent and embraced their role of getting the technology in place to support The Digital Campus. The VP of Finance and Administration, who saw the initiative as transformational, was on board but had a lot of fires to tend. The battle to win hearts and minds would be fought at the Department leadership level, considered midlevel management. I was reminded of the Harvard case study. Top leadership was committed (the President) but the Head of Ordinance, the mid-level manager, had killed the Winchester rifle from being supplied to the Union army.

Many important departmental priorities were fighting for political and budget support, making it an uphill battle for a long term, enterprise-level initiative. It was important to find common goals between The Digital Campus Initiative and the Departments. <51

If the Campus was going Digital, becoming a Place that would connect to the next generation of "always on" learners, four things would need to happen:

- an unrelenting commitment from leadership,
- real departmental buy-in,
- sustained funding, and
- a skunkworks team empowered to act.

The idea, when presented as a student success initiative, was well received, at least at the surface level.

I have hope, but not certainty. I'd give it time and see if the naysayers would

TakeAway <51
Look for Synergy

It will be politically easier to implement your initiative if you can create synergy between your innovation and other successful initiatives, particularly those with highly influential stakeholders.

TakeAway <52
Big change almost always takes a while

Be persistent but don't push when it won't help and may even damage your effort. There are times in the process where you need to wait for things to develop, for people to come to your point of view. Keep the fire burning but know your innovative initiative will not always be at the forefront of the key influencers thinking. Be Patiently Persistent.

become advocates. I moved into the *"be patient mode"* hoping for a spark to cause the initiative to catch fire. <52

35 AN ENTREPRENEURIAL STARTUP

If I was looking for something to move quicker, it would likely be something outside of the institutional bureaucracy, maybe working with a *Blank Sheet* again. As luck would have it, I got a call from a young lady who was looking for my advice and counsel on launching an internet based start-up.

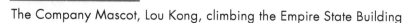

She lived in Seattle, one of the nation's leading innovation communities. The home of Amazon, Starbucks, and with Microsoft just a few miles up the road in Redmond, it was a hotbed of innovation. In addition to these giants, there were lots of new stars being born. Her startup needed some guidance and I'm pretty sure I knew why I was on the top of her list. I had the expertise and a passion for the customers being targeted – Architects. But maybe just as important as my expertise and passion for a new company working on a shoe-string budget, she was counting on me working cheap. Why? Because I was her dad.

The Company Mascot, Lou Kong, climbing the Empire State Building

We had our first consultation call the day after I had gotten the quick overview. It went on for about an hour, long for me. I'm not much for the phone, I like face-to-face meetings so I can *read* the body language. Anyway, the phone conversation filled in a few more blanks. She would have some in-house guidance in the tech area – her husband had a degree in Computer Science. My daughter had experience in customer service, holding jobs as help desk support while in college, handling the front-desk duties at a bed and breakfast, and managing the events unit at a Conference Center hosting 25,000 attendees a year. She was organized and good with people.

I believed she had the talent and drive to be an entrepreneur, but she was a little short on how to launch a business. That's where she was looking for my input.

"It's hard to tell with these Internet startups if they're really interested in building companies or if they're just interested in the money. I can tell you, though: If they don't really want to build a company, they won't luck into it. That's because it's so hard that if you don't have a passion, you'll give up."

Steve Jobs

I gave her my initial reaction – I was encouraging. Then I shared my 3 point, *Rapid Skills Development*, internet age business model:

- **launch your innovation with minimum up-front money**
- **move from concept to delivery FAST**
- **produce a revenue stream to fund ongoing costs.**

She needed my expertise in starting a business, and my professional knowledge – I was an Architect, but success would be up to her.

She wanted to sell digital downloads – and felt the online delivery of courses Architects needed to maintain their license would be a winner. I thought she had discovered one of the secrets to competing in a crowded market – offer a *got-a-have, not a want-a-have*. The courses she planned to offer were required continuing education by most States and the AIA (The American Institute of Architects is the national organization for the profession). This really rang my bell. I didn't let her know, but I was hooked. I liked the "secret *got-a-have*" formula, but I also had a personal reason.

TakeAway <53

Develop a business structure

If your innovation is likely to create a new business venture, put a structure in place as soon as possible. Establish the legal format, very clear roles and responsibilities of the participants, and the financial obligations and benefits. Plan for both success and failure. It's easy to put this off, but trust me, this is really important, you want to do this early.

I had seen my profession, Architecture, become overwhelmed with the complexities of modern buildings. Architects had lost their status as master builders and had been relegated to committee leaders, sometimes as just members of a Design/Build project lead by a contractor. I hated where the profession was going and had a burning passion to put Architects back in charge of creating the built environment. I must admit it was probably wishful thinking, but

Big things don't happen unless you think big.

I said let's start and see how it goes. I told her I'd be willing to serve in an advisory role and would send her a To-Do list – tasks that would need to be completed in order to create the business structure. <53

The To-Do list

- determine the credentials needed to be "Certified" as a provider
- see what State educational requirements Architects needed to maintain their license
- check out the competition
- get a handle on the price Architects would pay for courses
- take a look at potential marketing vehicles – Google Adwords, MailChimp, and other platforms
- determine who would develop course content
- estimate the cost to produce content
- determine the best format of the courses and web user interface
- estimate the time required to develop and maintain the web portal
- estimate the cost to put the content online
- determine the upfront cost before putting the online hosting infrastructure in place
- calculate the ongoing costs of doing business
- put together a 3-year cash flow analysis to project the Net Cash-flow
- decide on a company name and register a web domain

The list could have been longer, but I thought that was enough to get her going (or crush her enthusiasm). I sent the email and suggested we talk soon, maybe use Google Hangouts to check progress. She said great. How about in a week, two at the most? Seemed reasonable, and we set a time.

Two weeks later she said she was making good progress but needed a

TakeAway <54

Don't rush the research but don't plan forever

When you have an idea, do the research. But launch at 80%. You'll need to capture market share and build momentum. Be ready to solve problems as they come up.

124

little more time. I said, no problem; let me know when you're ready. I was not surprised, because with most good ideas, there's a lot to consider if you're going to turn your idea into a reality. <54

I got an email invitation to schedule a meeting for Sunday. It had been 3 weeks since she had shared her brilliant idea.

I was guarded and worried she had lost steam. It wouldn't be the first good idea that turned out to be fun to talk about but went nowhere. But I was pleasantly surprised. It seemed she had spent the time well. She had done her homework, addressing all the points on my list and even going the extra mile – doing some financial projections and learning how she

GROWTH PROJECTIONS

Year		2016	2017	2018	2019	2020
Total Architects	115,000					
Market Share as %		2%	1.5%	2.5%	2%	4%
Customer Growth		2,300	1,725	2,875	2,300	4,600
INCOME						
COURSE SALES		$20	$20	$40	$40	$60
TOTAL INCOME		**$46,000**	**$34,500**	**$115,000**	**$92,000**	**$276,000**
EXPENSES						
Operating Costs	25%	$11,500	$8,625	$28,750	$23,000	$69,000
Employee Salaries	25%	$11,500	$8,625	$28,750	$23,000	$69,000
TOTAL EXPENSES		**$23,000**	**$17,250**	**$57,500**	**$46,000**	**$138,000**
NET INCOME (50%)		$23,000	$17,250	$57,500	$46,000	$138,000

could get a national educational credential from AIA that all the States would accept.

She had also secured a domain name and created an edgy brand that seemed to fit a Seattle startup. I was encouraged. She said she was ready to apply to the AIA to become an approved provider if I was willing to let her use my Architectural license as a credential. Here we go – I could hear a sucking sound. If I committed to this, I was signing up to review the courses prior to her submitting them for approval. AIA required a registered Architect in the flow of the content development process. It seemed like a task I could do without taking too much time, so I agreed with a caveat: After the first year she would get an outside course reviewer.

She thought Architects Parti could become an approved AIA provider in 30 days and by then hoped to have 6 to 10 courses ready, the web-hosting provider selected, and the website tested and up and running. It sounded aggressive but I didn't let on. I decided to stoke the fire and said, "You can't go any faster."

"Stay hungry, stay foolish"

Steve Jobs

I loved her willingness to leap into action, to accept the ambiguity – having a plan but not being certain of how it would go. As Rhea had told me years before ". . . *always be bold enough to act when there is no guarantee of success."*

My daughter had also followed another rule I found imperative – *start with as little up-front money as possible.* This is a good approach for two reasons: If you're using your own money, it keeps your personal exposure low. Second, if you use investor's money, the less of their money you take, the more of the company you can keep. With the exception of course content, she had done all the work herself. She had a few Architects provide the content materials, with them agreeing to be paid out of the money generated as the

TakeAway <55

Shared risk, shared reward

If you have a killer idea and you've created a buzz, look for talent that will contribute their sweat equity for future profit.

courses were sold – a good way to limit up-front costs.<55

She didn't know what she didn't know, and I wasn't going to rain on her parade. She was organized, moving forward step by step. But a detailed, well-thought-out plan doesn't guarantee success. For now, I encouraged her to press on. We spoke a few times a week, tweaking the projections and refining the web-user experience. After 40 days, keeping our fingers crossed, she got the big news from AIA – Architects Parti was now included as an official provider in the AIA educational system. All AIA needed was a check for $850 to pay for the first year membership. For a start-up working on a shoestring budget, this was a big hit, but it was essential. The AIA credential made Architects Parti creditable to its potential clients.<56 She could now display the AIA logo on the website to highlight the companies membership status. The check was sent and the website was open for business.

TakeAway <56

Credentials validate your idea

Getting recognized by an established organization can make your initiative credible in the market.

The next big hurdle – Marketing. To start, I pushed her to get a Google AdWords account. It cost around $1.00 a click and you don't pay until someone views your homepage (again, no money up-front). But the website was only getting a few clicks a day. She refined the search keywords and got up to about 8 clicks a day. I reminded her, Architects Parti was an unknown commodity. She had established credibility with the AIA logo prominently displayed on the website, but traffic was still slow. At this point it was imperative to attract a lot more customers and, to be honest, she needed a positive sign soon.

After 9 days, lightning struck – the first customer. Someone had actually paid 20 bucks for a course! For her, and me, it was like hitting a grand slam in the World Series. There is nothing more important to an entrepreneurial start-up than customer validation, *especially* when they buy something.<57 And to boot, the system – from registration, course selection, payment, and finally displaying their Certificate to print – all worked without a hitch.

It was a start, but unless she could find a way to get more exposure for the website fast, somehow kick-start the business, she could lose faith that her startup would ever make a profit.

New clients continued to trickle in from AdWords. She kept improving the website, refining the user experience, and adding new courses. Business was steady but was not meeting the projected income. Expenses: AdWords, Web Hosting, basic overhead costs, even though they were pretty low, were still coming in. She needed a break. It turned out that the bureaucracy, mandates by the State, became an ally and shot the company into orbit.<58

One of the larger States had a special course requirement for all Architects registered in their State. After researching how to get one of these special courses approved, it looked pretty daunting. But even though she felt it was a long shot, she decided to take a chance.

After weeks developing the course with a content expert on the topic, getting it approved by AIA and the State, and paying an outside reviewer $400 (almost half of the cash she had left), the course was approved. During that same timeframe, the company got access to a database of the email addresses of all registered Architects in the target State, some 10,000 emails. Now she believed she had what she needed – the course and the target market.

She kept AdWords going, finding that every 12 clicks yielded a new client who bought an average of $40 worth of courses. So, for around $13, Architects Parti made $40, a net of $27. It was a trickle, but the margin was great and at least it was some activity.

She began an online marketing campaign, using the database to target the 10,000 Architects. Within a week, course sales went from 1 a day to 10 a day. It looked like the trickle was becoming a flood.

Find the Key for Exponential Growth

In a 2-month period, before the Architect's 2-year deadline to meet their educational requirements, total clients increased from 120 to 2,300. In the 60-day period before the deadline, three times the company grossed $3,000 in one day. Hitting that kind of mark in one day was almost as exciting as the day Architects Parti sold the first 2 hr. course for $20 (a hell of a deal – 1/3 the cost of the competition's average price). It was fantastic and, as the web system had worked with a trickle of customers, it now handled the surge in traffic with

TakeAway <59

Make your own luck

Initially you may not recognize what will be your big break or when it will happen.

Always keep your eyes open and be ready to seize the moment.

only a few small glitches. The system had withstood the flood.

I had coached her on how to put together the business plan. I had given her a list and she had done the research and mapped out what to do. But for one course in one State to redefine the company's market position, to make the ROI (Return On Investment) work, that was unexpected, some would call it luck.**<59**

This was a lesson I had learned before and on more than one occasion: You can have a well-researched, detailed plan, but "things happen." You need to be ready to take advantage of things outside of your plan. And she did.

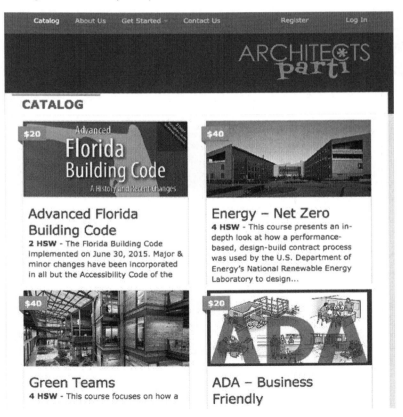

Architects Parti has been in the game for two years. It's still a one-person show except for me, acting as an advisor (a very active advisor with no course-reviewer replacement in sight). The company can now carry all its expenses plus afford to pay its one employee almost as much as she made in her last "regular" job. If things kept going well, she hopes to bring on some help for the next wave of customers.

After the surge in clients came a surge in confidence. Architects Parti 2.0 implemented a Full Featured website including AIA Credentials, a Custom Referral function, a web-based LMS, Instant Certificate printing, and a secure online payment solution.

The next 2-year cycle was coming soon that would likely generate a big spike in income. In addition, the national market was growing and the website's custom-built "referral" function was generating new clients at a rate that exceeded Google AdWords. The targeted email marketing was still the most effective means to reach prospective clients, but the company hoped the customers generated by the Referral Network would grow geometrically and become the key to expanding the company's customer base.

Architects Parti was rolling. But here's where I had gotten too comfortable, thinking a great start was all I needed for my initiative to be a winner. From Dream Home Designer to my Development project on the coast, I experienced

TakeAway <60

Be your most fearless competitor

When you think you're at the top of the heap, the dominant life-force on the planet, watch out.

Others have seen what you've done and are planning to offer a better mouse trap. They want to take you down and be number one.

Always be looking for ways to improve your product or service. Don't be complacent.

great success early while the final outcome was disappointing.

I couldn't let her get to excited and slack up. I gave her one last challenge – Don't start coasting, Ramp it up. Remember your goal is to be the number-one continuing education provider for Architects in America.`<60`

The online course Catalog had only 32 courses. To become the national leader, Architects Parti would need to offer a lot more courses – more like 100 to 150. One way to increase the volume of courses was to get more Architects to write courses for the company. But course authors typically get a big upfront payment or 50% of the sale price. With this approach, there would be more courses, but the income growth would slow. I wanted to explore another approach.

Would it be possible to cut the time needed to create a course? I suggested trying to get content from a different source – moving from the time intensive process of creating original materials to curating materials, leveraging existing web content that is not subject to copyright protection (content posted under Creative Commons license, e.g. materials on Wikipedia or Government documents).

Developing a new format to launch this curated approach was a tall order, but if the time to create a course could be cut by 50%, the sale price could also be cut by 50%. Assuming the same sales volume, the income would not suffer. In fact, it was much more likely that with many more courses and at a lower price, sales would increase.

Architects Parti was committed to offering quality Continuing Education, a core value of the company. But for the business to stay competitive and become financially successful, keeping prices as low as possible was smart. Within a few months the new format was ready and the first curated course posted.

Early feedback was good. Architects Parti had made a change and in doing so, stayed ahead of the competition.

I enjoyed my role as Advisor. I felt I had helped with the launch, and the StartUp was now a company with real potential. I would be available on call, but I felt Architects Parti was ready to move forward without my direct involvement. She needed to go for it.

36 A FEW FINAL COMMENTS

As I said in the Foreword, I never planned to spend a majority of my working life in bureaucratic organizations. And I certainly didn't intend to write a book about it. But I have.

In spending a considerable time in self evaluation mode, I've tried to pinpoint what drove me to be innovative. In a broad sense, I simply concluded it was in my DNA. But to be more specific, I connect my passion to innovate directly to my extreme curiosity and that I'm a bit audacious.

I've shared my story of multiple careers, distilling the *lessons learned* as TakeAways included in the side margins. The stories narrative style presents the flow of my career as an innovator. The TakeAways provide some insights that readers can apply to their own unique circumstances.

In addition to the TakeAways included throughout the book, I have presented five Essential Lessons that follow on the next few pages. Together, the TakeAways and the Essential Lessons are offered for guidance as you take on the challenges necessary to innovate within a bureaucratic organization.

Start with a creative idea and envision the process to make it happen

Innovation always starts with insights into something – a process or product you think could be improved or invented. It usually involves saving time, improving quality, or cutting costs. Sometimes all three. When you're ready to share your idea, you'll need to map out the innovation's implementation process, beginning with an in-depth analysis of what will help and also what will challenge implementing your initiative.

Get a firm grasp of the challenges you'll face by Studying the factors that shape the result

An innovation's implementation process is shaped by many specific factors: your level of expertise, experience, and authority; political and corporate relationships; the technology available; the time allotted; the quality desired; and the money budgeted. And one more factor you can't plan for, but can always count on – something unpredictable will happen – sometimes good, sometimes not.

Be ready to defy convention, resist blind compliance, always question the status quo

For your innovation to have impact, you'll need to propose an unconventional, maybe even audacious, solution. Don't comply with what's in place if you're convinced it could stand improvement. But remember – not everything needs fixing. There are times when things are working fine or may only need tweaking. But always be in the questioning mode, checking to see whether the status quo is worth preserving or is ripe for change.

Be relentless in your pursuit, determined to overcome resistance and build support

Don't lose your initial wild enthusiasm. Momentum will ebb and flow. Resistance can grow or subside. Change is never easy and seldom welcomed by those who must change. When people are comfortable doing what they're doing the way they've always done it, they'll first act as if they don't understand. After explaining your idea in a dozen different ways to blank stares, they'll shift tactics, finding a million reasons why what they're doing or using is fine and why your proposal just won't work. You must convert the naysayers to adopters and then to advocates. You must have an unwavering commitment to make your innovative idea happen.

Formulate a sustainability plan to insure The change will last for its useful life

For a new process to stick, and not be quickly replaced by the next new way, it must become the central nervous system of the enterprise. The new process must become integral to your better way of getting things done. New products also need a strategy to stay viable. They can quickly be replaced by copycats, cheap knock-offs, or someone's supposedly better mousetrap. A product will have the longest shelf life if it can retain its unique nature – while continuously improving in order to stay ahead of the competition.

I've been told on several occasions, Stop Tweaking – You're Done! And I really planned to conclude with the Five Essential Lessons just presented. But . . .

I can't help myself. I have to share one of my most memorable recollections and, in fact, where I got the title for this book.

The inspiration for the book's title came when I was attending a ceremony honoring Rhea's life. Many rose to share their emotional stories. But for me, her granddaughter captured Rhea's magic best.

"As all of you who knew her remember, my grandmother was someone who didn't con-form to convention. She had her own way, and it inspired me to think different. I re-member when I was younger, she was watch-ing me color, going slowly, making sure I stayed inside the lines.

She reached down, tore the page out, and said, 'color outside the lines."

That was Rhea –
Don't just color outside the lines,
Tear the Page Out!

Tear the Page Out

What it takes to Innovate in a Bureaucratic Organization

Written with *a little help from my friends*

Dr. Bruce Bickley

Professor of English, Emeritus, Florida State University.
Bickley and Associates, Professional Writing and Editing Instructor and Consultant

> Bruce was my editor and writing coach. He encouraged me to not lose my voice in writing my story. He made me better at the mechanics of writing, helping to unify the chapters into a story.

Sean Brown

Educational Technology Innovator

> Sean had a critical insight - identifying who my message was really for. Once I got focused on the right reader, my target market, it all started to flow.

Dr. Perry Crowell

Assistant VP of Finance and Administration, Retired, Florida State University
Adjunct Faculty, College of Education, Florida State University

> Perry always wanted a hard copy of each draft and gave me voluminous notes. After each reading he shared his thoughts, was positive and would say "you're making progress." He always left room for improvement.

Tom Martineau

Professor, Emeritus, FAMU, Architect, AIA, NCARB, LEED AP, President, Productivity House, Inc.

> Tom thought the content seemed factual but my stories didn't seem as exciting as he felt they were. His view was, if I wanted to inspire the reader, I needed to make the read more interesting.

About the Author

As a partner in a successful Architectural firm, Bill Lindner led the design effort to deliver thousands of multi-family living units, along with professional offices, shopping centers, and hotel projects throughout Florida. Building on his Architectural experience while working in diverse roles, he has applied his design and visualization skills to program development, project management, and organization reimagining.

As the Information Technology Director and then Deputy Chief of Staff for the Governor of Florida, Bill completely restructured Executive Office communications processes and re-engineered office operations.

Later, as Secretary of the Florida Department of Management Services, he applied the emergent computer technology and innovative program-management systems to streamline the internal services of state government – from facilities-planning and construction to tele-communications and purchasing. Bill eliminated redundancies, applied pioneering digital solutions to rethinking and restructuring complex systems, and dramatically improved services provided to State agencies and Florida citizens.

In the process, he created the High Performance Workplace that improved the productivity of thousands of state employees and led to Government Services Direct becoming the top-rated government website in the nation for two years running.

After leaving government service, Bill accepted a leadership position as the Director of Florida State University's Professional Development unit and directed the Office of Distance Learning during its four-year start-up phase. Bill dramatically expanded the delivery of online courses for both degree-seeking students and professionals looking to enhance their skills. He also led the building of the new FSU Conference Center, a state-of-the-art, hi- tech venue to host a variety of educational events, workshops, and conferences. Utilizing the web connectivity infrastructure, participants could "Meet in the Center, Connect to the World."

In the Case Studies presented, Bill Lindner shares his innovation adventures to help you design your own path to becoming a successful innovator.

139

Made in the USA
Columbia, SC
23 December 2020

29797235R00080